7 WAYS TO LEAD

7 WAYS TO LEAD

"When I think of leadership, growth, and impact my mind quickly goes to Andre Young and *You Evolving Now*. Andre is a man who doesn't just talk the talk, he walks the walk as well. The impact he's making in the world with his real-life lessons is immeasurable, transforming lives and businesses is just the beginning. This book is not only the evolution of Andre and his business but the evolution of leadership! Simple steps to change the direction of your business, your relationships, and your life, this is what's needed in the world."

— **Justin Scheck**, Founder of The Growth Now Movement

"At JULABO USA, our employees are more than just a number. Other thought leaders have created cookie-cutter approaches to their leadership and management trainings. Andre Young takes his training approach to another level. With the benefit of an outside perspective and experienced coaching skills, Andre is able to custom fit his trainings to match the unique situation of every employee we have put through his program. The ability to easily communicate with Andre about our needs made it possible to achieve the best desired outcome for the team. I trust my employees under his direction, and as a result, my employees gain more trust in me. This is how we evolve now together!"

— **Dirk Frese**, Vice President of Sales,
Marketing and JULABO USA

"I did *You Evolving Now* at my job. I enjoyed talking to Andre for 1-on-1 Employee Growth Training. I got a better understanding of my co-workers, my kids, and new things to talk about with my husband. I'm glad my job got in contact with Andre and did this for us!"

— Employee at *Snap-On Tools*

7 WAYS TO LEAD

Evolve Professionally and Personally
Enhancing Your Leadership and Work / Life Harmony

ANDRE YOUNG

NEW YORK

LONDON • NASHVILLE • MELBOURNE • VANCOUVER

7 WAYS TO LEAD
Evolve Professionally and Personally
Enhancing Your Leadership and Work / Life Harmony

© 2021 ANDRE YOUNG

Published in New York, New York, by Morgan James Publishing. Morgan James is a trademark of Morgan James, LLC. www.MorganJamesPublishing.com

Sales Rights: World
ISBN 978-1-63195-091-9 paperback
ISBN 978-1-63195-092-6 ebook
Library of Congress Control Number: 2020904403

Cover Design by:
Rachel Lopez
www.r2cdesign.com

Morgan James is a proud partner of Habitat for Humanity Peninsula and Greater Williamsburg. Partners in building since 2006.

Get involved today! Visit
www.MorganJamesBuilds.com

Contents

Acknowledgments

I am blessed to have so many people and experiences in my life to be grateful for. Thank you to my family and friends for your support, encouragement, inspiration, and wisdom.

Love and honor to my beautiful wife, Sarah, for your unlimited devotion through the happiest and toughest times of my life. Thank you for all that you are and for all of your 'behind the scenes' acts that support the foundation of You Evolving Now, LLC. To my children: Xiomara, André, Mason, and Sky. I love you! I am complete with you all in my life.

To my father, Robert, thank you for being my calming rock. Your words, sincerity, and patience continue to leave me in awe. To my mother, Sherri, "I love you" seems too simple a thing to say. Your truth has never failed me; even back when Randy and I use to barge into the bathroom just to speak to you! To my brother, Randy, I love you til the end. Many many thanks to my other family members and friends!

Lastly, a special thanks to my friend Ed Burns. Thank you for supporting my vision; recommending and motivating me to start writing 3 blogs per week so many years ago; creating an unstoppable passion and ability I didn't know I possessed.

Definition of Leadership & Work / Life Harmony

If you're reading this… you have an interest in living the life and lifestyle of your dreams. You are most likely a hard worker and dedicated to achieving your definition of success. As you read this book, your definition of success will expand as you learn how to EVOLVE as a leader (professionally and personally); enhancing your leadership skills, personal leadership, communication skills, and enhancing your Work/ Life Harmony! Before we begin… I'm a firm believer in the importance of defining the topics you'll be reading about and implementing into your life this book… Work / Life Harmony and Leadership! So, let's get to it!

You may have noticed I use the term, Work / Life Harmony instead of the traditional Work / Life Balance. The truth is… if we chase the strict line of balance it's easy to become frustrated, overwhelmed, and negative as things in life will only be perfectly balanced every now and then… and even then… not for long. Life is funny that way! So, instead of seeking balance in our work and in our lives… let's seek harmony in both. That can happen, can happen often, and the consistent thoughts, language, and actions we choose allow us complete control in both areas!

Also, Work / Life Harmony is more important than it's ever been in our society. The fact you have a cell phone; means your wife, husband, boyfriend, or girlfriend are now everywhere you are! If your relationships aren't good… you're at work, trying to do your job, while responding to ten pages worth of "Hate-Texts"! Vice Versa, when you return home… your phone continues to ring, ding, and chime with unending work emails, texts, and calls. Both areas of our lives, now more than ever, have to be as harmonious as possible; as they flood into each other nonstop! You're going to have fun throughout this book learning how to EVOLVE Professionally and Personally!

LEADERSHIP, what a big word! Over the years I have fallen in love with the positive impact a leader can spark… rippling through people, an organization, a team, within a family, and lives unknown to us… all based on one person's ability, willingness, and dedication to influence, impact, protect, and build! I began writing about leadership and working with companies, executives, employees, and athletic teams due to two major frustrations. One is the Promotion Process within most companies and teams, but we'll jump into that in Chapter 1. My second frustration stemmed from watching myself and others advance with promotions, titles, money, and things but failing to become any better of a person, partner, or parent! Knowing our craft and acquiring nice titles and stuff can be great, but is not everything and certainly not the only thing that will make you a leader.

I view leadership as two-fold and when I discuss leadership on stage, at companies and with teams I always start with the necessity and power of personal leadership… then the addition of great leadership skills! Let's first show up in our work, in our lives, and in our relationships in a way that makes people want to follow us; because they like, enjoy, and respect how we are and who we are… then we'll add some great, new, and easy-to-use leadership skills that we will later discuss in this book!

To make it simple, Leadership is the ability to Influence, Protect, Impact, Build, and Decide:

Influence

Can you influence people to be a better of the best version of themselves due to how you are as a person? Your ability to know your craft, convey a vision and message, connect with others... all others... not just the people you enjoy, move others forward together toward a common goal, and remain positive along the way... this is known as leadership!

Protect

At some point in our leadership, we will have to protect our people; our employees, our boss, our kids, and our partner. Sometimes, we may have to protect them from themselves... their bad habits, limited or lack of insight and foresight, impulsive behaviors, etc. If we've invited the right people into our circle, professionally and personally, this won't be necessary often but it will come up!

When I was an employee, I loved when a leadership team believed in me and believe me when something off-kilter occurred. Perhaps a customer/client complained; the leader would manage the relationship with the customer/client, but I was innocent until proven guilty... instead of guilty until proven innocent... and left the Follow-Up Meeting feeling trusted, respected, valuable, and with new information on how to address the problem or anything like it in the future. We can do this with our employees, our kids, are partners and choose to be a Leader that protects their value, their character, and their desire to stay committed to the vision.

Another example... there's an individual on your team that always comes in late. A leader knows... What's allowed in the beginning will be expected in the end. This person hasn't lied about who they are... they're late and late often. How do we protect this person from themselves... allowing them to leave the conversation feeling valued, motivated, and committed to the vision and new expectations?

From a personal and parental perspective, I am blessed to have four children; my youngest son's dream is to play in the NFL. He has the ability, the work-ethic, and fortitude, but this one thing gets in his way... FORTNIGHT! You parents out there (depending on what year you're reading this book) know what I'm talking about! He will wake up; without brushing his teeth, eating, or anything and BOOM... is on the game... with no pause button, engaged with his friends, and is eternally consumed. So, in being a leader in my home and protecting him from himself... we had a family conversation, the kids shared their dreams, and their personal daily plan to achieve their dream.

At night, my two boys (my oldest is out of the house and youngest was only 5 weeks old) agreed to hand over their PlayStation controllers, headsets, and cell phones. These items would be returned the next day once they woke at the time THEY established, brushed their teeth, ate real food, completed chores, exercised, watched a motivational video, and worked to develop their craft (making 25-50 shots in basketball). If this took an hour... so be it! If it took three hours... so be it! Funny thing is... it's amazing how quickly it all got done, how much better they were for it, and it all stemmed from being willing to protect our people; not only from the dangers in society... but from themselves!

Lastly, we must be willing to protect our people from us! You know your bad habits, how you are when you're in a bad mood, stressed-out, tired, or simply hungry! A leader is in tune with their psychological and emotional state and careful not to let a negative state drip into the team. As leader's we must also stay vigilant not to burn-out our "Inspired & Motivated" people (employees, teammates, athletes, kids, etc.); which you will read about later in the book. Just because they are eager, capable, and willing doesn't mean they should DO and BE everything; while others within your organization or team get to DO and BE less!

Impact

What impact will you make in the lives of those following your lead? If we've led right, at some point those individuals will experience a moment when they look back and remember something you've said or done that made a positive life-changing impact in their lives! How many of those moments will your name and memory be attached to?

Build

Leaders build! We must build and expand our dream, our vision, our knowledge-base, our abilities, and our people. To many organizations and teams will tear down and destroy great and willing people due to the use of terrible language, unrealistic expectations, ridiculous workloads, and simply not enough human kindness and empathy! We must build our people with what I call "Construction Talk" as well as the ability and willingness to speak everyone's language. By the end of this book, you'll be able to speak everyone's language on the planet with my Leader's 7!

Decide

Leadership is a verb; therefore, leadership is a decision! We must decide to become leaders; in and of our own lives. We must choose to show up in our lives, our work, and our relationships with a positive attitude and willing to DO and BE our best. The rest of my 7 Ways to Lead will explain how… and add some necessary, but easy-to-use leadership skills on top of it! Let's get started and enjoy your EVOLUTION!

"Leadership is a verb; therefore, leadership is a decision!"
— **Andre Young**

WAY TO LEAD 1

A LEADER'S PREPARATION

CHAPTER 1

Lead to the "er"

Although the title of manager, boss, captain, etc... all imply leadership; I think we can agree they are vastly different from true leadership and BEING a Leader. Unfortunately, so many are elevated to the positions of authority due to their ability to achieve in a singular area. A person sells a million dollars' worth of product; they're promoted to Sales Manager, a player scores hundreds of points; they become the team captain... I can go on and on! Perhaps they do have true leadership skills, but all that is evident at the time of their promotion is the ability to do that one thing well. They haven't proven they can lead anything or anyone!

In Contrast, so many seek manager or leadership positions because that's where the money is, or security is, the titles are... you know, the "American Dream"! In all fairness, I suppose it would be difficult to turn down an opportunity for advancement, more money, more prestige... only to see someone you feel as less qualified get it and then have to bring that story home to your husband, wife, and family. In a perfect world… this wouldn't matter and your company/job would pay you or reward you more for the job you really want to do, are great at, and we could all stay where we wanted. The great thing is… if you are the person that is content where you are OR the person ready to climb the ladder; it's important to understand we are all leaders. We are first must be willing to effectively lead our own lives as a Person, Professional, Partner, and Parent!

As a leader, our job is to focus on two little letters… "e" and "r"! At the end of a word or at the end of a description of someone or something… these two little letters are powerful and will either represent decline or progression, rise or fall, disappointment or triumph. Either way, that "er" represents MORE in either direction and it's our job as leaders to influence the positive "er". Back in my "Athlete Days"… I wanted to be bigg"er", strong"er", and hit hard"er". As an employee… I wanted to be smart"er" in my craft. As an entrepreneur… I wanted to be a bett"er" influencer. It bothers me to this day how long I waited to share my dream of wanting "er" in my life and failing to seek mentorship; as so many of us attempt to go at success solo for various reasons.

True leadership is about mentorship; mentoring people to achieve their definition of "er " in their life. Are you managing or mentoring your staff? Are you parenting or mentoring your children? Are you coaching a team or mentoring your players? Mentoring their "er" implies we will positively influence their thoughts and behaviors as we teach and set examples that will never be forgotten and passed on to people they know; creating a legacy of "er". Mentoring implies we will make an impact that changes the way they see themselves, their superpowers, and how they can and will impact the bigger picture of their company, team, family, and life! So, how do we do it?

Curiosity

Typically, the first time we are ever asked why we want the job, or want to be on that team, or go to that school, etc. is the last time we're ever asked! Our initial interview for the job, school, or team tends to be the last time curiosity exists. What are the dreams of your employees, students, players? This question is prevalent in elementary and middle schools, but unfortunately begins to fade into obscurity the older we get! If their dream is outside the lines of the team or business... is this ok? Can it still be valued? Supported? Cheered and Celebrated? At the minimum, asked about and encouraged?

When I wrote my first content-based book... my baby... *7 Ways to Love* I worked part-time as a mental health therapist, part-time as a salesman, and full time in my business. It was an odd time of life as I was running a company with 12 staff, figuring out what I was doing business-wise, working two other jobs, building a house, and being a family man. The great thing was... The sales store I worked at was connected to a Barnes & Noble in a strip mall. I would make a sale, send the customer over to buy my book, and they'd return immediately for me to sign it at a terminal! Not only did my job support my dream... there were other staff in the store that had hidden dreams of becoming writers and no one knew it. I was able to become a leader and mentor a few awesome men that I value knowing to this day!

As I sat in a job interview for my final ever job as an employee; I unapologetically shared my dream of being a speaker, author, and Founder of my company; You Evolving Now, LLC. I was in the midst of blowing my company up and I knew it was going to take off in a few months but, in the meantime... I had bills to pay and needed a job. I shared my dream, my situation, and promised I would be the best employee they had... from the hours of 9-5... and meant it with all of my heart! I had employees... so I knew what they were looking for in terms of employee mindset and effort... but I never wavered from my dream and neither should you!

The company was awesome and I am thankful to them for taking a chance and hiring me. Sharing my dream made me work even harder as not to make a fool of myself and still be there years later with a sob story, but more importantly… it allowed them to know me, my desire, and ask me about it frequently! I'm not saying this approach will work the same for you; I'm simply sharing the positive side of it for both myself and the company… as I still speak highly of them to this day!

Permission

Permission is simple. Some people and YOU may simply need permission to "er"! Some employees, players, students, dreams are bubbling right below the surface… only waiting for a kind and encouraging word of permission and belief! Wouldn't it be great if your words were the ones to set them free? So many companies are scared of losing great people. Statistically, you're going to lose them anyway; wouldn't you rather have great people positively impacting your team and culture for a while and leave a remarkable impact… rather than the dejected "Dream-Hider" that's now bitter and blaming the job and team for holding them back. We all know the negative impact that builds… now multiply that over weeks, months, years and decades!

Celebrate

As leaders, once we know someone's dream and give them permission to fly… doesn't it only make sense we celebrate their successes? It's awesome they did great! If and when it's time for them to move on, it should be of no shock; leading them to their "er" allowed you to know who they were, their passion, their ability, their plan, and your plan to move forward as well. Upon their departure… ask them, "Who do they know that would be a good fit here?". Who could they kick back your way? When this person leaves… this is a positive, vibrant, and influential person… how do you want them speaking about you, the team, your organization out in the world?

All of this may sound simple, but I can guarantee you it's not and is missed in many organizations. People ask me, what do you talk about as a speaker? My response is Work / Life Harmony and Leadership… Common Sense Leadership! There are many great consultants focused on Organizational and/or Strategic Leadership and there is a huge necessity for that, but my focus is Common-Sense Leadership; allowing individuals to positively lead their own lives in their 4 P's and create the most awesome life of their dreams at work and at home "er-ing" all the way! Who will you help lead to their "er"?

As you continue to read, when I talk about leadership; it's two-fold. Of course, learning the essential leadership skills beneficial to make an impact on your dream and goals, but also how you positively choose to lead and live your own life! How you consistently show up with a positive mindset, a servant leadership attitude, expanding the vision and intentionally building-up others through impact, influence, protection, and expectations for greatness… That's Personal Leadership! The next few chapters will explore your journey to "Personal Leadership"; making it easier for people to follow you because they enjoy and respect who you are and how you are!

> *"How you consistently show up with a positive mindset, a servant leadership attitude, expanding the vision, and intentionally building-up others through impact, influence, protection, and expectations for greatness… That's Personal Leadership!"*
> **– Andre Young**

CHAPTER 2

The 3 Other Marriages

For so many young men and women... finding the right person is an essential part to solidifying a successful life. The right person that gets us, completes us, and allows us to achieve the dream of getting the house, the family, and success! Although, this process is not for everyone and has been delayed by a number of years due to continued education and prolonged independence it's still a dream for a majority of people. As great as this process is and can be... there are 3 other marriages that get looked over and are essential to becoming a leader, in and of our own lives and leading us to the real experience of success! So, what are they?

Marry Yourself

Back in the 1990's, you may remember Dennis Rodman, a famous NBA player for the Chicago Bulls. He became known for the outrageous; his hair color, his fashion, his behavior on and off the court, and one particular incident of marrying himself! He arrived in horse and carriage and decked out, head-to-toe, in a white wedding dress and blonde wig to a church to marry himself. Many were in shock as the event unfolded, but as I watched it I couldn't stop thinking that he was a genius! The wig and wedding dress wouldn't be for me, but the concept of Marry Oneself had never entered my mind before that day.

At some point, many of us will stand at an altar of some sort and give ourselves to another person, make vows to the relationship and that person, and hopefully live those vows out until death do you part. But... when was the last time you've made vows to YOURSELF, to YOUR life, and to YOUR dreams?

We all get ready in the morning and brush our teeth in front of the mirror to head out to win the day, but how many times do you make intentional eye contact with the person in the mirror? I remember the day I married myself... like any other day, standing in front of the mirror getting ready... I felt compelled to make eye contact, maintain eye-contact, and make some vows to me. I vowed not to fail, to reach my definition of success, to go deeper and also be a success as a husband, a father, and friend. I vowed to live my dream of supporting my family with content I created through my own business and to live our desired lifestyle as a family! What a powerful moment that I will never forget and use as daily motivation!

What vows will you make for yourself, your life, and your future?

Marry Your Dream

Most of us have dreams... dreams for our life and what we want to have. I encourage you to go further and also dream of who you want to be and how you want to be! When I ask most people their definition of success or what their dream is... they tell me the one thing they believe that if they chase it hard enough and catch it will make them happy. I hope everyone achieves their dream and being a Dreamleader is the cherry on top of any relationship. However, the typical one-perspective answer I receive is limited and dangerous… because one of three things will happen to your definition of success:

1. We will achieve our definition of success, but not be the person we need to be to keep it or enjoy it.
2. We will achieve our definition of success, but it's not what we thought it would be; leading to feeling unfulfilled, depressed, and lost.
3. Or… we achieve our definition of success; we are the person we need to be to enjoy it… and life comes and gut punches us and changes everything!

So, be sure to Marry your dream… but also know what success and your dream look like in your 4P's as a Person, a Professional, a Partner, and Parent; so when your original definition of success changes or is taken away by life… YOU are still great!

Marry Your Why

What you want is good to know… "Why you want it" is even more important! Our "Why" is who we are, our motivation, and what will be needed in the tough times as a leader when we'll need to reflect on why we are doing all of the hard work that our desired lifestyle, our dream, and our relationship/s take.

Remember "Why" you went into your field, your relationship, etc. Prepare yourself… as sometimes your "Why" may change. It doesn't have to be for better or for worse… it simply may be different. If you choose to stay on the path… then appreciate the positives your "Why" offers, smile, do and be your best, and manage the negatives by eliminating complaints about what you can't control and doing your part in what you can control!

*"Marry your dream, but not the path you think will get you there...
or more dangerously the path you think you deserve!"*
– Andre Young

CHAPTER 3

Get Your Triangle Right

I n this frantic pace of life, it's easy to let the daily duties of the day become more important than living a more EVOLVED life. It's easy to let your life, your kids, your job, and the day take over. Now add this up day by day after day, month after month, year after year, decade after decade… how can happiness, joy, love, and relationships win?

We are all busy in our own way… throughout my time as a marriage counselor and CEO of You Evolving Now, I've encountered numerous men and women and hear the same thing. Typically, men pridefully say and defend themselves with, "I work, work, work". Women tend to say with pride, "My life revolves around my kids". Do you know where they said this… in counseling with their marriage hanging by a thread or already over. Work is necessary, but cannot be the only thing that brings value to you or the relationship. I'm sure your kids are amazing, but what does your partner hear, when you say "My life revolves around my

12

kids?... That they are not important, can be pushed aside, put on hold, and are irrelevant. So what to do?

Let's get your triangle right! Imagine a triangle... at the top is your vision and expanded definition of success; as well as your faith. If you are a faith-based person and your faith helps you to be a better person, have a better relationship, and live an honorable life... that's at the top. If you are not a faith-based person... As leaders within your relationship and of your own life; talk with your partner about your dream and vision for your life, lifestyle, relationship and family. This is what guides you... not the kids, not your job, and not the duties of the day. What kind of relationship and lifestyle do you both wish to have and want to enjoy? This is how we begin to ensure true Work / Life Harmony!

On the bottom-right side of the triangle is you and your partner; and other important relationships. Your partner is the person you have chosen, love, and respect... remember to cherish, love, respect, date, and care for each other... and make sure your kids witness it! Is your significant other in your calendar? Yes, the calendar you have on your phone... that you can set alerts and reminders to. Are your kids in your calendar? Your friends? It certainly doesn't sound spontaneous, but too many times... the important people in our lives get pushed aside by either our "Busy" or our laziness; negatively impacting our Work/Life Harmony and our ability to effectively lead our own lives!

On the bottom-left side of the triangle, is YOU. It's necessary to care for yourself, treat yourself, follow YOUR dreams, and live your best life. The kids are not forgotten... they are in the middle of your triangle. All points of your triangle will revolve around them filling them with love, lessons, and direction.

If your job is at the top... what happens when that job goes away? If your children are on the top... it breeds entitlement, parental servitude, and... eventually, the kids are supposed to leave one day. What will it be like ending up in a house with someone you've neglected for 20 plus years? They may no longer be the person you remembered... add resentment, possible dissatisfaction and/or lack of interest... and you have a recipe for disaster. So... get your triangle right and EVOLVE!!!

CHAPTER 4

Follow the Leader

L eadership and winning get much of the glory in our society. People who possess the desired leadership qualities to motivate, inspire, and guide themselves or others to success are highly valued and even more highly paid. Leadership is a wonderful quality to possess as it infers that you are passionate, super-knowledgeable, able to connect with others, inspiring, and motivated. With all that said... leaders and leadership are important, but so is following!

Much is never said or ever glorified about following or followers. It's often deemed as a negative to be a "Follower". Shouldn't that depend on who or what YOU choose to follow? The truth is, when you don't know the way, it then becomes imperative to make wise decisions on who or what to follow. Following the right way requires patience, understanding, and thick-skin for leaders. It takes intelligence, decisiveness, motivation, diligence, trust, and a lot of want-to in order to achieve your desired goal and arrive at any desired destination. Following is not for the faint-of-heart and the decision to follow the right thing, person, or path… needs to be respected and has proven to build and enhance the leaders you know today in the areas of business, sports, etc.; as they all had their "hero" and if they were really lucky… a Mentor!

Sometimes as a leader… you will find that you don't know everything; you must be aware and humble enough to know that you don't know… and choose wisely who to follow. However, as a follower, you must know when to use your own wisdom, when to set your own path, and enhance your leadership. Value your role as a follower as much as your role of leader; being willing to learn, EVOLVE, and build!

We will play both, the Leader and the Follower within the roles we all play as individuals, professionals, partners, parents, friends, teammates, and more. It's impossible for us to know everything…the wisdom of following the right thing or person will prove necessary. Enjoy your journey!

Who do you value as a Professional at your job? As a person overall? As a parent? How will you begin to follow; stealing what they do well and adding it to your arsenal to become a better leader?

CHAPTER 5
Be a C. E. O.

What comes to mind when you think of the title CEO? Some think of the fitted suits, board meetings, managing, and of course... the money! Hollywood has depicted quite a picture of what a CEO looks like... and this may be true in some aspects. Other CEO's may wear jeans and operate their business out of a messy garage... nothing like the picture you have in your mind. The truth is... it doesn't matter what a CEO (Chief Executive Officer) looks like... what matters is how they lead, the impact they make, and the progress achieved due to their existence, knowledge, efforts to connect with others, and fulfill the needs of not only their customers... but also their people! The great thing is... you can become a CEO today... right now!

Success begins with our ability to lead... and that starts with being able to lead ourselves. I encourage you to become the CEO of your own life! Take charge and build YOU to your best self, health, wealth, and lifestyle at home, work, and in your relationships as a partner, parent, son/daughter, brother/sister, friend, etc.! That's a lot to take in... so where do you start?

We start by thinking and living C. E. O.; Care, Embrace, and Operate! Growth is greatly stunted in the presence of fear; and greatly enhanced in the presence of care, self-care, and belief in your own ability, vision, mission, and your team. You must begin to care about YOU! Invest in yourself by brainstorming your dream and expanded definition of success in your 4 P's. Build your confidence and a team around you to motivate, inspire, and hold you accountable.

E—Embrace the obligation and duties of your dream. Being a CEO has its perks, but the daily grind of focus, managing, problem-solving, connecting, keeping the faith, and bouncing-back is exhausting and will break the weak-minded! Embrace the daily grind that will make you successful: waking up earlier, reading more, learning more, possibly going back to school, learning how to relate more effectively to others in your life. Whatever the grind is that relates to your dream... embrace it until it becomes routine and more easily conquered.

O—Operate! This is the action phase of leadership and your success. Caring and embracing are mental and emotional obstacles... Operating is doing! Schedule your day, create a list, check things off... focusing on daily growth as well as vision and plans for the future. What is your vision for your life a year from now? Do you know your partner's? Your team's? Your people's? Does your daily operating agenda address this vision?

A new position of C. E. O. has just become available in your life. Either you will accept the position... or, you can let the other 3 billion people on the planet take it from you. Believe me, they can't wait to be your boss, tell you what to do, and take control of you in your 4 P's! Maybe this person is your boss, your partner, your kids, or any of the countless strangers you pass in a day. Either you will become the boss, leader, and C. E. O. of YOU and for others or someone else will!

"Success begins with our ability to lead... and that starts with being able to lead ourselves."

– Andre Young

CHAPTER 6

Newly Appointed Leader?

Are you a newly appointed leader, about to be, or want to be? What a mix of emotions; from being excited, nervous, ready, not feeling ready enough, wanting to make an impression, wanting to make changes, but how many... and the list goes on! Whether you are going to be a new leader at your job, on your team, or in a home and in your family... here are a few things to help get over the hump and allow your EVOLUTION and success.

As a young aspiring leader, I remember my first promotion. I was ready... or so I thought! I had the vision of what I wanted to achieve and the knowledge base. To add... I was being promoted to supervise my old co-workers and friends... Wow! So, there are positives and negatives to everything... In the previous sentence, I stated I had a vision of what I wanted to create and how I wanted everyone on my team to be. The positive is, I had a vision... great! The negative is... in my vision, everyone had to be like ME! Let's first remember... your team are PEOPLE not titles, they all got to where they are and their positions because of their own superpower and gifts. Yes, it will be a great addition to their arsenal to have your skillset, but they have their own. As Newley Appointed Leaders, how do we accept their gifts as assets and add to their arsenal allowing your team EVOLVE? Let's get into it!

Vision & Expectations

As a new leader, what is your vision for the team, company, family, etc.? Are there other leaders above or below you that should have input on this? Vision is important... communicate it to your team, share how the team can and will get there, ask for feedback and ideas... not complaints, negativity, or story-telling (as your people may have been along for many rides of so-called "leadership" and have great ideas that may be useful).

A vision is nothing without expectations! When it's your vision for your life alone... you will manage all of the expectations, but this is a team. Everyone must know what the expectations are. Sometimes the hardest thing to do as a new leader is to stay consistent with the expectations; as your head is spinning, wanting others to like you, not wanting to make waves, or wanting to make too many. Either way... it's tough! Through my company, You Evolving Now, I often do 1-on-1 Employee Growth Training Sessions on-site for companies and teams. The most common complaint I hear is... expectations are not followed and people get away with it. Once vision and expectations are set and then broken repeatedly... this becomes the culture. It's hard to get your team to follow with all of their heart, effort, and energy in an inconsistent or consistently apathetic culture.

Tip: Before, during, and after implementing your vision and expectations... be sure to get to know and "build-up" the individuals on your team and the other leaders around you! Kind words, pats on the back, a smile, and "Thank Yous" go a long way and are more important than you can imagine!

Who are They?

Who are the people on your team? This is broken down into two parts as a Newly Appointed Leader.

1. What do they want in a leader? What's important to them? Why are they on the team? What's the hardest and most frustrating thing about their job or place on the team; along with their suggested solution? What's the best part of their job and why? We rarely, if ever ask these questions. On a job, these questions are typically asked in the initial interview regarding their previous job... then you'll see this employee again in 12 months for their annual review... where they get a list of numbers to sum up their yearly effort. This cannot fly; if you want to be a leader... do this more regularly!

    Tip... if you, as a leader, ask these questions... it means you are tough enough, mature enough, and ready to hear any answer without defending or disconnecting for the purpose of understanding, improving, and EVOLVING!

2. As a leader, what are your people's superpowers? As a young leader, I didn't care... as I said, I wanted them to be like me, care like me, and have my superpower. But, their superpower got them where they are, not mine! Mine will enhance them, but let's use theirs and put them in the position to make an impact. Perhaps it's giving them a task that fits their superpower, allowing them to head a project that fits them, maybe it's a position change, an opportunity to conduct a training on what they do best, or to train YOU on what and how they do things, creating a new position for them, etc. I call this, Right-Seat Leadership! Are your people in the "Right Seat" to help the company, team, or family? We'll get more into this later in the book!

Tough Teaching & Learning

This is the T. from my Lead with H. E. A. T.! No leader is exempt from this and our vision will fail if we cannot do this. At some point, an employee, athlete, student, friend, or child will test the line… some will toe-test over the line… some will pole vault over the line; and believe me… all of the silent by-standers are waiting to see what will happen. What is done in the beginning… is usually expected in the end. You do nothing as a leader… that same "nothing" will be expected in the middle and end! So, let's soften the blow that is inevitably coming.

I was a therapist for 17 years before switching paths, becoming an entrepreneur and starting my company. This one simple conversation made my job so much easier and I still use it today. As I met my clients for our initial session… we spent time getting to know one another, along with what they wanted to get out of their time and experience sitting with me, but lastly… I'd end with… "I look forward to continuing, but at some point down the road, as your therapist, I may have to say some things that are hard for you to hear, but are a part of me doing my best job and helping you get to where you said you want to be, is that going to be ok?". Every time, 100% of the time, my clients looked at me and said ok. "That time" may have come 2 weeks later of 2 months later, but when it did… I simply said, "Remember that time when I said I would have to say something that may be hard for you to hear? They would respond, "Yes"… and I'd say, "Are you ready?". 100% of the time… they took a deep breath and let me hit them with it!

I don't promise you my 100% rate of success. I also don't promise they or the situation will change 100% of the time. This simply sets you up as a leader… setting the stage with honesty and anticipation that good and bad will come. You have prefaced it, introduced it, and shared it with respect. You have done your part… you wouldn't need a team if you could do it all yourself. Allow for the tough teaching and be ready for the tough learning! Later in this book, we will go more in-depth on this topic!

"As a Leader... Vision without expectations is just hope. Expectations without consequences are merely suggestions."

– Andre Young

WAY TO LEAD 2

A LEADER'S GRATITUDE

CHAPTER 7

Avoid the "I have to..." Trap

If you want to be successful, at some point you will have to choose to give yourself some credit. It always amazes me how many people shy away from credit, pats on the back, deflect compliments, and so forth. You are an amazing person that makes a million great tiny decisions per day; making you the person, professional, mom/dad, husband/wife, and everything else you are! Our success will be found in our choices and decisions... but also in our language!

Most people dig a "Have-To" Hole so big by 11:00am it's no wonder why they can't stop feeling overwhelmed, trapped, defeated, controlled, and abused! It all starts when we wake... "I have to go to work", "I have to meet those deadlines at work", "I have to pick up the kids and take them to their practices, games, and the 30,000 other things they're involved in after school", "I have to spend time with my partner". The truth is... you don't have to do anything. YOU choose to and continue to choose to do it... and your continued decisions to do what is right, necessary, and beneficial for you, your family, and your life is a big deal and needs to be celebrated! However, the language of "I have to" helps to create the trap I discussed at the beginning of this paragraph. The words we put into our heads and in our lives will impact how we feel, then what we do, followed by consequences; either negative or positive. So, what to do?

What if you transform your language... allowing an EVOLUTION of perspective and gratitude? Instead of "I have to"... try... "I get to". Not many people are in your position in the world and would trade places with you in a heartbeat for what you have, who you get to be with, where you get to live, the job you get to complain about, the children you get to have, and the life you get to live! I don't say this to minimize anything you may be currently going through; however, I say it because it's true! The fact that you can read this book, bought this book, and possibly reading it on an iPad of some sort is amazing... ask someone from a Third World or war-torn country struggling to eat, struggling to protect their family, and working in a sweatshop? I know that's extreme, but it exists and is going on right now and not to you!

"I get to go to work"... you know the place you interviewed at, were excited to get the acceptance from, and can quit anytime you choose. "I get to go to work" sounds and feels a lot better than, "I have to go to work". "Tonight, I get to take my kids to basketball practice" sounds and feels better than "I have to take my kids to practice". Most importantly it positively impacts our brain... forming a more positive thought, leading to a more positive feeling, more positive behavior, and more positive consequences. People with miserable attitudes were not born that way... it was a series of negatives and constant negative thinking, leading to negative feelings, then behaviors, stemming to ongoing negative consequences that keep the negative wheel spinning.

Yes, this little trick will be odd and at times seem crazy to apply... while you may be cleaning toilets at your job or preparing dinner for the 16th million mundane time, but what do you have to lose; compared to what you will gain? Make the change verbally and let those around you hear your new language and see who you inspire over time. If it's too weird for you to say aloud… simply catch yourself saying the old "I have to" and change it in your head to "I get to". I use this simple switch toward gratitude to this day and it still works wonders; reminding me of how lucky I am to live this life I've created for myself!

"Leaders don't "Have to", They "Get to!"
        – Andre Young

What do you "Get to Do" today?

CHAPTER 8

On Our Death Bed

Throughout your life, you will have many scary moments in which you narrowly escaped trouble, big trouble, or even death. One second earlier or a minute later… could have been that accident or awful situation that changed everything. These moments make you feel lucky for a brief period of time… as there is nothing more humbling and enlightening than a true near-death experience to WAKE US UP!

On February 12th, 2013, I felt ill but thought nothing of it as I simply charged ahead to win the day. I toughed through what I thought was a common cold and stomach ache; as I oddly never get sick. I woke on February 13th, 2013 still feeling a bit out of sorts, but had a big day at work and was excited to make an impact with a family I was working with. However, by 10:00am, I could tell something was wrong… a very different kind of wrong. There was a pain in my stomach I couldn't explain and I've never felt before… and never want to feel again! I was in mid-meeting with a family and suddenly pushed myself away from the table to excuse myself from the meeting and work all together. I decided to head home but struggled to drive; as my commute at that time was an hour. The pain grew worse and worse; causing me to contort in the car as if I were going through an exorcism. The swells of pain were excruciating!

I finally made it home. I'd never been so grateful to see the entrance of my house. Upon struggling with my keys and entering my home all I could do was collapse on the floor. I laid there for a while; allowing the pain to subside a bit. Being way too "macho", I decided to make my way upstairs to lie down for a bit to tough it out. Luckily, a friend called… simply to say hello, but wound up saving my life. (Mel, Thank You so much and I owe you one… a big one!). He happened to be in nursing school at the time, asked my symptoms, and told me to get to the hospital immediately! I called my wife and she wasted no time leaving work to take me to the Emergency Room.

After crawling into the hospital entrance due to the pain and unable to stand… it was the busiest emergency room ever… all I could do was lie on the floor in and out of consciousness. The pain on a scale of 1-10 (10 being the worse), was a 30! I was improperly triaged and laid on that floor for 6 hours… sweating from the swells of pain, in and out of consciousness, and suffering. As I laid on that hospital floor, I knew something was really wrong. Between the swells of pain, in-between states of consciousness, and an unwilling triage team… all I could think about were two things… "Does my wife know how much I love her" and "Did I teach my kids enough that I could die right now and they'd be sad… but they'd be OK; due to what I've taught them". I remember telling my wife I loved her and calling each of my kids from that floor and saying… "I love you… do you remember what I taught you?".

I somehow summoned the energy to beg the nurse that was ridiculing me for lying on the floor for pain medication… only to be ignored a few more times, but finally taken to a back room. It was found that my White Blood Cells were WAY out of whack… and a long story short… I had a Perforated Ulcer, my kidneys were functioning at 20%, and I was literally dying. I was rushed into emergency surgery and woke the next day in a hospital room. Every doctor and nurse I saw during my stay shared how I was lucky to be alive… and I must agree!

I am lucky to be alive and so are you! The big and little things we worry and stress over all day will not be on your mind when you're on your death bed. What will be on your mind is… TIME, FAMILY, and LOVE… not money, success, your phone, Facebook, Candy Crush, and all of the other bull crap we make important and all-consuming! Did you spend your time enjoying your life, experiencing life with the people you care about, and contributing to meaningful work? Did you love hard, beautifully, and correctly? Did you teach your kids enough about you, life, and enough to carry them through life without you around? EVOLVE and become a leader in the areas of how you spend your time, love, and how you manage change. If you can do this… YOU will have lived the life of your dreams!

CHAPTER 9

T. G. I. T.

Y ou may be more familiar with T. G. I. F.... Thank God it's Friday! Everyone loves a Friday... it's easier to get up on a Friday, it's the last day of most people's workweek, and no matter what happens... it's Friday!!! If you work a traditional 9-5, Monday through Friday... simply observe the difference from every other day. People are smiling more, a little bit lighter, a little less gets done, and people are in a track stance at 4:59pm ready to sprint out the door, to their, cars, and start their weekend! The truth is two-fold... 1. Many people are eager to sprint away from work and to a home, relationship, and life that they have just finished complaining about all week and feel unfulfilled in 2. Although Friday's feel great... there is value in all days and every day! Why can't it be T. G. I. T.... Thank God it's Today! This is what leaders say!

T. G. I. T. has nothing to do with what day it is... it has everything to do with you, your mindset, gratitude, joy to meet the day and all it has to offer, and beat the day instead of it beating you! YOU get to rise today and begin your day... some people didn't! You get to go to the job you applied for. If you hate it, change your perspective or start looking for a new one! You get to spend time with your significant other today... at some point, you won't... so, how will you enjoy him/her today? You get to spend time with your kids... whether through the craziness of their young schedules, over the phone, or Ubering them to and from practices and games... enjoy them... You had them... they didn't ask to be here... and should not have to feel like a nuisance or be told how much of a burden they are on a regular basis.

T. G. I. T. works better when we choose to focus on our lives; inside and outside of our jobs. Nothing hits harder than life; you may have taken some of life's hardest hits and have given up on certain aspects that make life worth living. Some people have given up on relationships and say "I'm just all about my kids", or work, and have seemingly shut down and surrendered to the idea that this is as good as life is going to get.

That's not LIVING!!! And at some point, the kids are supposed to leave... and we all know your job can change or be downsized in the snap of a finger... just like your life. So... get up, start leading your life, be a leader to and for others, and T. G. I. T. your way to the life of your dreams!

"T. G..I. T. has nothing to do with what day it is... it has everything to do with you, your mindset, gratitude, joy to meet the day and all it has to offer, and beat the day instead of it beating you!"
– Andre Young

CHAPTER 10
Gunpoint?

Over the past few years, I have made a disturbing observation that both frustrates me and fuels me. I encounter countless employees that act as if they were awakened at gunpoint to come to the job that they applied for. This spans amongst all professions; doctors, nurses, athletes, retail, check-out clerks, etc. As an employee, how many of your co-workers begin the day with a sigh and grunt as if they would prefer to be anywhere else than the only place that is paying them to be there? Of course, this is not for every employee or co-worker... anytime you say "All" or "Every", you're wrong; but the majority can be draining!

There are a plethora of reasons why you as an employee or your employees arrive at this point: lack of interest, lack of growth, lack of opportunity, perhaps they grew and the job did not, life issues, poor management, and so many more. Can you remember a time when you were at a store or restaurant and an employee provided you with excellent service, a smile, connected with you, and made your day? If you answered "Yes", you walked away impressed with them and their ability to make you feel special; to the point you may have even asked to speak with their supervisor about how good they were and your experience with them! Well, that could be you today as an employee, employer, and leader!

The truth is... you applied for the job you're at. Your boss or coach didn't barge into your home this morning, wake you at gunpoint to go to work, and force you to do the job you so actively searched for, completed applications/resumes for, interviewed for, and get paid from. Abraham Lincoln said it best, "Whatever you are, be a good one". So today, be a "Good One"! If your current employment or team is no longer for you... that's ok and can be viewed as a great opportunity to start the search for your new passion and dream!

"When your passion becomes your work and your work becomes your passion... your life will get great!"
— Andre Young

WAY TO LEAD 3

A LEADER'S
CONFIDENCE

CHAPTER 11

Stop Allowing an Average Life

Life is amazing, life is odd, life is a lot of things! There are times when life will surprise us both good and bad... life can be fair and it can be extremely unfair at times. Good and bad happen to the good and bad alike. Although some things are out of our control... remember this, we tend to live what we allow!

You're in a relationship that you continue to complain about... what are you allowing in your relationship and your life? You're in a job you can't stand... what are you allowing at your job and with the people with work with? You're living the definition of an average life; droning through, no excitement, and bored... what are you allowing in your relationship and relationships, how your significant other or your kids treat you, etc.? It's easy to look at others, blame them, and say it's their fault... "If they...", "They should...", or "I can't...". All of this may be true, but if you want a GREAT or better life... it's time to do something different and become a leader; in and of your own life!

Different doesn't always mean better, but when you are sick and tired of being sick and tired, DIFFERENT maybe just a good enough path to a new beginning! To start your new path... you must first realize that if YOU want more, YOU have to be willing to DO more. If YOU are the one that wants different; you will have to be the one that is ready and willing to do and be different. So... DO more or different in your profession and your craft, DO more or different in your personal leadership and leadership skills, DO more or different as husband/wife/boyfriend/girlfriend, DO more and different as a parent; allowing enhanced personal-responsibility, self-awareness, increased opportunity, and EVOLVED Confidence that you can do more and be more in whatever you decide and dedicate your consistency to!

Doing more usually includes our thinking patterns, our actions, and an inquisitive approach to our new life as a leader. Having a great life and the life of our dreams will also depend on asking important questions to ourselves and others... What kind of life do I want; as an Individual, a Partner, Parent, Professional, etc.? When was the last time you asked your partner, "What would it really take for US to have the best relationship ever? What about your boss... "How can I be better here and make the best impact with what I have to offer?" or better yet, your employees... "What do you love most about working here and dislike most?". These questions and the answers are monumentally important! Even more so, is our ability to hear the answers without becoming defensive, argumentative, and destructive to yourself and those important relationships.

Actively living a great life is not for the weak! It takes risk, inner strength, determination, self-love, and respect for ourselves and others to live the life of our dreams. It's a good thing these all exist in YOU! You can choose to take this journey as fast or as slow as you'd like. But, today is your first step! Whatever you do... if it's your passion... make sure to do it daily, do it smart, and do it to the best of your ability! Enjoy!

"You can DO more and BE more in whatever you decide to dedicate your consistency to!"

– Andre Young

CHAPTER 12

A Leader's Confidence

I remember starting my business back in 2011 with a few friends and interested individuals in my living room. Who knew it would EVOLVE in helping people live their best lives as leaders in companies, schools, and online around the world... I didn't! There were times when I was going to quit due to lack of sign-ups and commitment from interested parties... but, never from a lack of my desire.

I even had family and friends encourage me to quit... or at least make it a hobby. **_Quick Tip..._** if you have friends and family tell you the same thing about your goal or dream... it doesn't always mean they don't love you, believe in you, or care about you. Sometimes... it's the only way they know how to care. They can never know the true passion you have for your dream; as they are set and quite comfortable in their path. So, they think they are helping you, protecting you, and caring for you as they watch you struggle, vent, and claw your way inch by inch. If you have the guts to move forward toward your dream...

what you'll need is CONFIDENCE! And at times that can be in short supply.

In my closet, there is a sticky note… it's the first thing I see getting dressed every morning… and it says CONFIDENCE in big bold letters! Sometimes, you will be the only one that believes in you… and that will have to be enough as you do these 5 things!

Marry Your Dream and Your Why

This is YOUR dream and no one has to or can love it like you! Stop wasting time being angry at people who don't understand or support you and start finding and maximizing your time with the ones that do! Marrying your "Why" allows you to focus on your dream and your "Why" rather than the path you think will get you there, the path you want, or most dangerously… the path you think you deserve!

My "Why" is helping individuals in their 4 P's in my own way and with what I have created through my experiences, past training, and my own concepts. My initial path was signing up interested people in the community to come out in the evening and EVOLVE while participating in my Men Evolving Now and Women Evolving Now Forums. I still love the idea, but it wasn't a fortuitous business plan as it became difficult to compete with people's "Busy". Whether they were busy working a second job, carting their kids around, making dinner, or elbow-deep in a bag of chips… it was their definition of "Busy" and it became too frustrating to compete with! Marry your Dream and your "Why" but remember to allow the path to wiggle and squiggle… that's where learning, growth, and EVOLUTION occur!

Consistency

Anything you do often… you'll get better at. They say practice makes perfect. That can be true, but an awfully slow process. Rather… Perfect practice makes perfect! You want more confidence? Do the right thing in an intentional manner consistently! Initially, I was very opposed to writing and only wanted to make videos to share my message. A friend strongly suggested I write to boost my SEO's on my website and write 3xs per week. "Oh no!". But, I was married to my dream and did it. Now... 4 books, writing for a magazine, a local paper, and you reading this book... I can't stop or even imagine not writing. Consistency... Leaders are consistent!!!

Head Up/Eyes Up/Smile

I attend a slew of sporting events as both of my sons play both football and basketball and I always look at body language. Particularly, the athletes that come off the bench. When they enter the game... where are their eyes, their heads, and their body movement? The confident player enters the game with their eyes up, making eye contact with other players and opponents (no fear... only excitement), head up, and moves quickly and decisively to where they are supposed to be. The player that does the opposite quickly identifies themselves as the weak link and a player to be exploited. If I can see it from the stands... don't you think the other players and opposing coaches do too? So... how are you entering the game, your dream, your job, your goal! Head Up, Eyes Up, and Move with Purpose! Even if you make a mistake... make it moving full speed, with purpose, learn, adjust, and EVOLVE on the way!!! ***Quick Tip:*** *Remember to smile. A smiling person achieving their goals is way more inviting and attractive!*

Perform

Our confidence and Dream will eventually come down to results. We may all have a different timeline on when we'll alter or stop our dream based on results. At some point, I was forced to stop chasing my dream of the NFL due to age; as my aggressive nature and "linebacker heart" was suck in a cornerback's body. My ambition didn't match my confidence in a new position, and my body simply struggled to stay healthy. But, I made it further than most and have many great memories. In contrast, the dream of my business had no boundaries and I knew I would never stop. However, I chose to work two full-time jobs for 7 years before I could walk away and only do my dream. I chose to turn down promotions and higher pay… to focus as much as possible on my dream. At some point, how we actually PERFORM will make all the difference and bump us up to where we want to be!

Performance will entail us working smarter… as well as harder. The hard work never stops! Performance will come down to you knowing your craft and how to make an impact; allowing you to become the leader you can be proud of and that people want to follow. Consistency, knowledge, and the ability to perform will boost your confidence and reduce your prep time. ***Quick Tip:*** *Reducing your prep time is not the only goal… use your gained time to learn new things that will take you to the next level!*

"What would _____ do?"

We all have role models. Someone we admire for who they are, how they handle things, and what they've achieved. If you don't have a role model… I encourage you to close your eyes right now and think of one! When we don't know what to do or are dejected, or things are great and we are thinking of the next step should be… simply ask yourself, "What would _____ do?" and begin! This person can be famous, your pastor, a co-worker, or neighbor down the street. ***Quick Tip:*** *It's as important to think of the next step when things are great… not only when there's a struggle.* Nothing stays the same for long… things are either slowly getting better or worse. As a leader, you control the flow with your dedication and forward-thinking! Ask Blockbuster Video… if you're old enough to know who they were, you get it! If you don't know who they are… that's my point.

"Head Up, Eyes Up, and Move with Purpose! Even if you make a mistake… make it moving full speed, with purpose, learn, adjust, and EVOLVE on the way!!!"

– Andre Young

CHAPTER 13
Leaders can be Insecure?

Insecurities... we all have them, but yours alone yells the loudest in your head, in your heart, and within your relationships at work, in your home, and in your personal life. We've all been impacted by life and our past is not always pretty. Some parts of our history and relationships have left marks; along with personal thoughts and feelings related to how we look, what we have or don't have, our position, or lack thereof; impacting our ability or inability to be the best leaders we can be. Our past negatives and how we choose to view them will either help us or hurt us... So, let's do something about it!

It's important to remember that your insecurities are YOUR insecurities and need not be given to other people: your significant other, your kids, or your staff. They are yours and need to be addressed by YOU! So many times, we enter into relationships or a new phase of life and expect that person, that position, the promotion, or the power of success and money to fill that void and provide us with the self-worth that only we can give ourselves through the power of EVOLVING our thoughts, perspective, choices, habits, our definition of success, and our ability to connect with others.... In other words, your Personal Leadership!

Yes... that job, that position, new opportunity, or new relationship feels great in the beginning and has you on Cloud 9, but tough times and obstacles are always just around the corner. Be proud of YOU for being in the positive and awesome situation you're in, but with insecurities looming... danger is imminent and tends to look and sound like this: you struggle to believe you are worthy of the position, opportunity, or partner... So, you eventually begin to test. "Am I really cut out for this?", "Why do you love me?", and/or you may begin to create situations that disconnect you at work as you stay in your office; failing to connect, or become overpowering and dominate.

In your intimate relationship, you may constantly test their love and affection; behaving poorly to test if they will stay. The problem is... If your partner leaves... it makes you right that you are unlovable; ultimately continuing the negative cycle. Or, they stay; chipping away at your respect for them... and you continue to test. Neither option allows you to live the life of your dreams or become a leader.

So how do we begin the process of overcoming our insecurities? We must first be aware of what our insecurities are and why they are. What are you insecure about? What or who makes your insecurities rise? Who or what are you comparing yourself to? Are your insecurities situational? You may feel insecure due to your weight, the amount of money you make, your inability or desire to live up to the definition you or someone else has given you about the various roles you play as a CEO, Vice President, Manager, Husband/Wife, Parent, Bread-Winner, Parent, etc. Realize these are all definitions society, media, your past, others, and YOU have put into your head. What kind of leader do you want to be and how do you mix your superpowers with what is needed?

Second, acknowledge where you are and who you are. This includes your positives, negatives, and what you personally bring to the table as a Person, a Professional, a Partner, Parent, and more... and take pride in it! You don't have control over everything, but if you don't like something about YOU... either accept it or change it! Whether you choose to accept it or change it... find your positives and celebrate it... no one wants to hear you whine, complain, or self-degrade yourself. It's unattractive and proves to be an exhausting full-time job for others to constantly fill a hole that only you can fill.

What are your Superpowers? How do they positively impact your work, your relationships, and YOU? Now that you have your answer... maximize your Super Power and perfect your craft so that your name becomes synonymous with your power and promote it wherever you are and with whomever you're with. Of course, it doesn't hurt to add to your skillset, but every successful person and company first found a way to do one thing great before they expanded into other avenues!

Finally, enjoy your life, live your life, and actively work to build-up those around you. You will be surprised how much you will receive when you decide to give and more importantly... "Build-Up" your team, employees, leaders, partner, kids, and your friends!

"It's important to remember that your insecurities are YOUR insecurities and need not be given to other people: your significant other, your kids, or your staff."

– Andre Young

CHAPTER 14

A Leader's IMPACT

Whether at our job, on our team, in our family, or in someone's life... We can all make an impact and positively change lives! You may have this desire buried deep inside of you or it may be right at the surface eager to burst out... but how do we do it? Some people are natural "Impactors"; while others may not have the natural flair but have the desire. The good news is... anyone can make an impact and here's how!

We must first understand that making an impact is different from making a difference. Anyone and anything can accidentally make a "difference" and that difference can be for the worse of for the better. The keyword was accidental... someone can accidentally say the right or wrong thing or that car running the red light can accidentally make a big difference in your life. When you say someone made an impact in your life... it usually implies a powerful, thought-provoking, action-oriented event that led you to EVOLVE as a person and be forever grateful!

Remember, making a difference can be good... but making a positive impact is better!

Making an impact will first start with you *Choosing to be Positive*:

If you're a naturally positive, smiling, wide-eyed person... this may be easy for you. If you are not... the work is remembering to be POSITIVE. The easiest thing to remember is... there are positives and negatives to everything. Find the positives quickly and operate your thinking centered around them; choosing to live in your positives throughout the day! As our thinking goes... our feelings follow, then our actions, ending with life consequences... either positive or negative! Yes, the negatives still remain... The trick is to manage them; splitting them into two categories.

If the negatives are in your control, then find a way to manage them to work them in your favor or simply accept that they exist... and because you've been reading this book and focused on enhancing your personal leadership and living your best life in your 4 P's... you don't need everything to be perfect or go your way for you to be a great leader! If the negatives are out of your control... find you peace with them, move on, and vent appropriately. Making an impact doesn't mean you'll never get upset or need to vent. It does mean that your venting isn't for everyone and anyone who'll listen. Make sure your venting is people-limited and time-limited for the sake of moving forward and EVOLVING!

Remain Humble

If you're to impact others... chances are they like and respect who you are and the lifestyle you are leading. By their definition, YOU are a success... and success can have a funny way of going to our head! Your job is to remain humble as you are impacting the people at your job, on your team, and in your family. There may come a time when you fall from grace and they may be the one impacting you... be sure a "big head" doesn't leave you the only one in the room!

Be Willing

Carry yourself with head up, eyes forward, smiling, positive, and humble... you will begin to attract people looking for impact. You will not have to come to them as the proof is always in actions, not in words. They have been watching you... and when they're ready... they will come to you! When a person comes to you for guidance, mentorship, and leadership... you must be WILLING to listen, meet them where they are, be honest without being rude, and helpful. This process is the art of impacting!

If the previous step is an art form...
this final step is a Science... Construction Talk!

I mention this in my book, *7 Ways to Love*, as one of the most important concepts of relationships and personal leadership. The premise of *Construction Talk* is to always be building! As a leader, when you're talking with someone it's important for you to keep in mind... you are either, building them up or tearing them down? If they have sought you out and are now in front of you seeking advice or direction... many times I find most people are seeking permission to follow their dreams. It's your duty as an Impactor to complete the process of listening, meeting them where they are with understanding, being honest without being rude, helpful, and ending with ENCOURAGEMENT that they can and should follow whatever they are passionate about and willing to put the work into!

The beauty of this is... it works everywhere! If you are a boss it works with your employees, a coach, a teammate, in your family, with friends, and with strangers. EVOLVE your confidence as a leader by EVOLVING someone else's!

> *"Making a difference can be good... but making a positive impact is better!"*
>
> – Andre Young

CHAPTER 15
Setting Goals and Keeping Them

A s you read this… you may be in the best place, head-space, and having the time of your life. If you are… great for you! This is what I call, Have-it-All Mode. You're achieving your definition of success and living the lifestyle of your dreams… I've been there! Or… you may be in the worst place, confused, and struggling in so many areas and aspects of your life. I call this… Survival Mode… I've been there too! No matter which mode you're in… it can become difficult to dream, set goals, and achieve them. Why?

It's hard to dream in Survival Mode as the walls always feel as though they're closing in and everything is a "Must", urgent, and life or death for the sake of survival. Perhaps what's making you feel that way is your job, maybe your relationship, your kids, money… or a mixture of all of the above. No matter the combination; it's difficult to dream when we're simply trying to survive and possibly feel broken at the same time.

It can also become difficult to keep dreaming and evolving when we get to the top of Success Mountain. You finally made it; you caught and earned whatever it was you were chasing... Only to have this empty feeling of... "Is this it?" or "Now what?" and have no answer. If you've never experienced this... believe me, it's a real thing and if you have experienced it; you know exactly what I'm talking about. The interesting thing is... the same things (job, relationships, money, and kids) that can lead us to Have-it-All Mode can also lead us into Survival Mode. The trick is to stay a leader and keep moving forward, but how do we do it?

Our dreams are our fuel! Our dream is the energy and spark that makes life fun, purposeful, and pulls us out of bed in the morning! Your dream must be your long-term vision... the goal is then your short-term solution... that fuels and dictates your daily action! So, first... what is your dream? This refers to what you want out of life? What makes your heart sing and is your passion to do? What would you do for free because it brings you that much joy and satisfaction? Now, be mindful and let's expand your dream! What's your desired lifestyle as a Professional, a Partner, and Parent (feel free to add more roles: sibling, son/daughter, etc.)? What big and small goals will it take for you to get there? The smallest goal can be YOUR starting point!

It's important to remember... YOU cannot start your dream and your dream does not exist without your vision AND some "Make-Yourself-Do- Itness". Yes... I made up a word! Let's face it... "Want To" is great, but not many people WANT TO wake up early for their goal, do the daily grind of their goal, or the obligations of their dream and goal. That comes later... after a bit of success is achieved! To start, "Make-Yourself-Do-Itness" is what you'll need! No one can give you this, there is no book to read, no special seminar to attend... YOU will either start doing something new, different, more, and consistent or not!

Whatever your goal, passion, and dream... remember to Do it daily! Be sure to put your goal into your daily schedule. This allows you to make it a habit... therefore, making your dream a habit, making your success a habit; therefore making your evolution a habit! Place your new goal into the calendar on your phone, set alerts and notifications, making you choose to ignore the growth you said you wanted! Make and Take the time to do what you know will make you feel good about you and see how your daily, monthly, and soon to be yearly wins begin to compound; sparking an evolution in how you think, feel, and behave!

Lastly, be willing to celebrate your EVOLUTION! Be careful not to take your upcoming small victories for granted! Accept the compliments from others, become a "Dreamleader" for others, and continue to develop new aspirations for yourself and your life! I once overheard an odd conversation while doing an Executive Coaching session at a company. Two women were talking about accepting compliments and one woman said… "I don't take or accept compliments; I feel that anyone that does is full of themselves". I was blown away and even more blown away as I heard the other woman agree with her. I'm not putting this on women or one gender; as I've heard similar things from men. My point is… when insecure meets confident, they will usually mistake it for conceit. Not accepting a compliment for something you've trained for, practiced for, struggled for, and value in your self would be a crime against yourself. Be mindful not to make yourself feel small so that someone else can feel comfortable or big. Enjoy and celebrate what you're achieving and who you are becoming and shine when you enter a room!

Tips to Achieve Your Goals:

- Make them visible: Put them on your bathroom mirror (My Favorite!), your phone calendar, reminders, etc. Your dream needs to become your weekly goals; and your weekly goals dictate and become your daily actions!
- Change your language: No more "If I…" or "Try". Use "When I…", "I am…" and other positives-based words!
- Be an intentional learner: learn about your dream and goal. The more you know about it, the better your process will become!
- Get an Accountability Buddy or Team: Meet or call regularly to discuss your goal with a mentor, friend, or success-based team.

• Seek and Utilize daily motivation and inspiration: Perhaps your faith or spirituality can play a part in your dream. Also, use sites and leaders such as You Evolving Now (non-shameless plug!) or social media outlets focused on empowerment and growth to provide that consistent spark or kick in the pants!

"Not accepting a compliment for something you've trained for, practiced for, struggled for, and value in your self would be a crime against yourself."

– Andre Young

CHAPTER 16

Success is a Language

Did you know, You Evolving Now began because of language? Actually, for a lot of reasons, but language was a huge one! I became so frustrated and turned off by the amount of negativity and pessimism exclaimed on a daily basis; people complaining about the weather, their job, their relationship, and their life. Enough already! What you think, affects how you feel, then what you do, and the consequences thereafter. So, no thank you to the negativity... leaders invite the language of success into your life!

There are certain words that act as thieves and bullies and need to be removed from our vocabulary if we are to become leaders. The main culprits are: "But", "If", "Can't", "Try", "Just & Only", "Should", and "Deserve". Lock them up and throw away the key... and here's what to replace them with:

"But"—We all know that anything after "But" is...! It robs you of sincerity and accountability. Example... "I'm sorry I hurt you, but..."

Compared to, "I'm sorry I hurt you, it was not my intent and it won't happen again" Which would you prefer to hear?

"If"—Implies doubt and doubt can lead to less than your best effort. Here's an example... "If I have the house of my dreams" compared to "When I have the house of my dreams". "If I make it to the NFL" compared to "When I make it to the NFL". "If I get the promotion" compared to "When I get the promotion". Which sounds better? Be mindful not to negatively mind-speak yourself out of your greatness; as you will perform better the more you believe in yourself... and every word towards your dream counts!

Some will say... don't put all your eggs in one basket with the "When I...". I agree 1000%; while still using "When I..."! The trick is to speak your success into existence while also "Expanding your Plan A!". Here's an example: What would you like to do after playing in the NFL, after getting that promotion, after achieving that dream? Great, let's focus on that too and expand Plan A. This allows leaders to evolve their interest and roles outside of the one thing that means the most to them right now.

I use this with athletes and executives. So much focus goes into achieving and advancing; it can be easy to forget there's life happening during and after success! Note: if you are raising an athlete... Be Mindful. So many people, coaches, and parents are well-intentioned Dream-Killers; sharing the statistics of those that make it compared to the number of those that don't... The "Your only one injury away Speech". This speech wouldn't happen if they told you they wanted to be a doctor, or get that high paying job, etc.

The discussion can sound like this... This is your dream... great! How can I help you? Let's say you play 20 years in the league and end with more Championships than Tom Brady... you will still retire younger than I am now. What else do you want to focus on so you're ready when sports are over... whether it's 2 days from now or 20 years from now? Great... let's do that too! This is the difference between Dream-Building and Dream-Killing! Besides... who the heck ever wants to settle for Plan

B? Do you want your Plan B life? Your Plan B husband or wife? Your Plan B job? So, be a leader and start building your Expanded Plan A Life right now!

"Can't"—Implies you are incapable of doing something. In some cases, this may be true, but in most cases, what you mean to say is… "This is really hard for me" or "I don't want to do _____". These are truer statements and both are OK!

"Try"—Have you ever invited someone to an event and they responded, "I'll try to make it"? Do you expect them to be there? No! The same way you don't expect them to show up is the same way your brain and soul feel when you say you're going to TRY referring to your dream. "Try" is our polite way of setting yourself up gently for failure.

"Just" & "Only" are Bully words that completely minimize who you are and where you are in life right now. It sounds like, "I only go to Community College", or "I'm just an executive Assistant". The truth is… If I or someone else said you were just a… or only a… you'd be so offended you'd probably want to fight!

Allow your truth to be the truth; acknowledging and accepting who you are and where you are in life right now… and letting your motivation, dedication, and willingness to become more speak for itself! "I go to Community College and I'm going to _____" or "I'm an Executive Assistant and my plan is to _____". Accept the path, enjoy the path, and know you are more than "Just" and "Only"; being mindful not to bully anyone else with these curse words!

"Deserve"—The final and most ego-pumped word on the Bully List. At some point, we have all worked hard to get to where we are; personally, professionally, and relationally. Some of us have worked hard for a little while; as others have an on-going drive to best themselves, achieve their dreams, and desired lifestyles. If this is you, good for you and I am truly happy for your successes! The important thing to know here is… Once we add the word "Deserve" to anything; it involves our ego and rarely has involving our ego ever made anything better.

Saying what we think we deserve is not a problem within itself; rather it's the feeling of righteousness that ensues as we say it! It pokes our chest out afterward; "I deserve that raise", "I deserve a man/woman that treats me good", "I deserve a promotion". These may all be true; what is truer is… "I want that raise", "I would like a man/woman who treated me more the way I want". Or "I want that promotion".

What is also true is… you didn't get it! Instead of wallowing or having a tantrum in the "Deserve" Pool… let's understand why it didn't happen, what factors (yours and outside factors) are contributing to the disappointment, and what's your game plan moving forward? The positive forward game plan is the key… as unfulfillment in the "Deserve" Pool tends to lead to you shutting down or ramping up. This looks like the worker that becomes significantly less productive, inefficient, argumentative and/or insubordinate. The player on the team that is running slower, half-heartedly going through drills, and engaged in side conversations with teammates or doing their own thing and arguing with coaches and other players. This is the spouse that becomes distant, disconnected, cold, and flat or easily agitated, argumentative, and unsupportive. "Deserve" is a dangerous word… replace it with "I would like _____, how can WE/I make it happen if possible?".

CHAPTER 17

How to Live B. O. L. D

B OLD... what an amazing word! Seeing and even saying the word makes it almost regal; as you respect someone that is BOLD, lives BOLD, and willing to accept the consequences of their BOLDNESS; either positive or negative. Years ago, I did my own 7 Ways to Love Homework and wrote a list of 25 things I loved about my wife. I placed it somewhere she'd find it and to my surprise... Days later... I saw a hand-designed card on my desk. It was a list of 25 things she loved about me. I can't remember all of the wonderful things she described... but I distinctly remember one word... "Bold". I remember feeling so proud she saw me as "Bold"; as for me it represents strength, determination, conviction, honor, and leadership... and contrary to many opinions... "Bold" doesn't have to mean off-putting, loud-mouthed, or disrespectful. It simply means doing, saying, or standing up for your passion and dreams in spite of popular or more powerful opinions. So, how can you live a more BOLD lifestyle in your 4 P's?

B—Be Brave

We all have our own Bravery Meter. You don't have to be as brave as anyone else, but your life will EVOLVE as you begin to take a bit more... or a lot more action than you're typically comfortable with. Many of us prefer not to rock the boat in our lives, our jobs, and in our relationships. It's amazing what we can allow ourselves to become comfortable with! Bravery may mean saying something different or being willing to do something different for the purpose of EVOLUTION. Remember... if you are the one that wants more or different; you will have to be the one that does more or different. Your bravery may not always make things your definition of "Better"... but different will ensue and sometimes different is all we need for opportunity to catapult us into our new lives... and THAT is brave and bold!

O—Optimistic

There is no point in choosing to live Boldly if you're going to be miserable the entire time! Be optimistic about the change and evolution you're creating. Everything has a negative and positive. As you live B. O. L. D., change will occur... and you will do best when you decide to live in your positives and manage your negatives.

What are the positives of your current job, position, and lifestyle? Awesome... let's intentionally enjoy them! What are the negatives? Ok... which negatives can you control? Which are out of your control? What's the plan for those you can control? Now... stop worrying about the things you can't and have faith in your actions, intent, and willingness to EVOLVE and change as necessary. Leadership!

L—Live above the BS

This is huge... and what will make you truly BOLD and not like the others! Living B. O. L. D. isn't just about saying what you want, when you want it, and how you want it. It's also about our self-control and being capable of knowing when and how to react.

As you live B. O. L. D.… not everyone will be ready for or enjoy will your change. Your friends, partner, kids, boss, employees… may not like it or be ready for it, but it's here now… So, what to do?

We can discuss our changes and what we'd like or need; not in an entitled sense of what we feel we deserve (that's a bully word), rather out of our growth and desire to expand. Discuss what you'd like to do different, why, and discuss a plan and the willingness you have to take the step together as a team. It's great if your job, your partner, kids, etc. are willing to change and EVOLVE with you… but, it's not always likely others will change at the same time you do or be ready for growth on your timeline. YOU be the change and remain positive while doing it!

Finally, understand restraint. As others are not ready for or enjoy your change… they may have hurtful things to say. Every action DOES NOT require an equal reaction! After explaining yourself time and time again… sometimes the best thing is to offer acceptance. YOU accept them for being how they are, where they are, and what they currently know. At this point, you must intentionally add the type of people, places, and things in your life that match your evolution so you are full and not drowning in your old life and your old self! People, relationships, and jobs change at different rates… perhaps one day, their change will allow you to cross paths again with no hard feelings… and that may be difficult if you parted ways looking down on them!

Note: We are all human and at times our emotions will win. In those moments… allow your message and delivery to be correct; so you will have to apologize for how you said something. If you can't hold back the venom… Apologies are not above true Leaders and we will get into a Leader's Apology later in the book!

D—Determined

There is no B. O. L. D. living without determination! Be determined to live your ideal and best lifestyle! What's the alternative… misery, drowning, and droning? You are your patterns… Be mindful!

"It's not always likely others will change at the same time you do or be ready for growth on your timeline. YOU be the change and remain positive while doing it!"

– Andre Young

CHAPTER 18

The 5 Points of Your Day

L eaders know there is a huge difference between dealing with your day and winning the day. As I've conversed with various people in schools, colleges, and in the workforce; there are so many people "dealing with their day", trudging through, complaining about things they knew were coming, and exhausting everyone they come into contact with... spreading their negativity and gloom. It's as if someone barged into their homes, roughed them up, put a gun to their heads, and made them go to school, to work, or to their job; forcing them to be successful. We can all agree that this didn't happen! If your coach or employer is coming to your home and waking you at gunpoint... please alert the authorities! If you are the coach or employer strong-arming your people... stop the madness immediately!

All jokes aside... Remember, you chose your university, you chose that job or promotion, to start your business, be in that relationship, have that family... then remember to act like it... and win the day! It's up to you to strive to be the best person you can be, EVOLVE in all the roles you play, and make an impact wherever you are and for whomever you may meet.

How do you win the day? Wake with positivity and a vision for your day. Do you have a goal you'd like to fulfill? It could be as major as closing the biggest deal of your life. Or as simple as connecting with people throughout the day regardless of the outcome. As your day progresses… avoid the drainers, negative people, and toxic conversations. You know them… the conversations that revolve around how bad, stupid, or horrible someone's day is, the weather is, the job is, or their relationship is. Choose to comment with either a positive or simply excuse yourself from the interaction. A simple trick I use is… "What's been good today"? It encourages people to find the good; now you both have an opportunity to discuss positive things and congratulate one another. This will become contagious as they will look forward to your next encounter and expect positivity. The Negative Nicks and Nancys will become easy to detect as they will have nothing to say and will eventually avoid you and run when you arrive.

Embrace every role you play and all the transitions of your day… You can go from professional to parent, to husband/wife, and back to professional very quickly. Embrace the role and transition! Not many people are as lucky as you to have so many roles and people that value them. Throughout your experiences today, keep your eyes open and take everything in. What can you learn? Who can you learn from? What will you do next time? Finally, end your day on a positive… read something positive, watch something funny, have a different type of conversation with your partner (One of the biggest reasons I wrote my book, "EVOLVE"); there is no reason to stop learning about the person you spend the most time with)… then… wake and repeat! Not every day is going to be the best day, but you can EVOLVE every day!

If you're hungry and serious about winning the day… here are my 5 Points of your day to become intentional about:

1. Wake putting something powerful, inspirational, and motivational into YOU, your mind, and your spirit! We all know what eating fast food daily at every meal will do to our physique... the converse effect is also true. Put positive things in your mind and spirit consistently and that will compound! On your way to whatever your work is... get your mind and language right by listening to motivation videos, podcasts, or yours truly; allowing you to walk into your work, school, and team life with a smile and ready to influence!

2. When you get to work, your school, or to your team... organize and prepare to win. You're there... might as well win and make the experience great! Make your "Get-To-Do" List, get your coffee, juice, or day-starter, make eye-contact and engage positively with the positive people there... whatever routine is best for you! Develop it, do it consistently, SMILE and enjoy!

3. Our Midday... there comes a time we can all fade and lose focus; especially if you're not in love with what you're doing. This is the time to intentionally do something for yourself and become mindful of who you allow to rent space in your head. Perhaps it's best to take a real lunch and enjoy it, go for a walk, visit a new place to sit or eat, only engage with the positive, text something awesome and sweet to your partner or kids, scroll pics of your family on your phone, or scroll positive and beautiful things on social media platforms. Take care of your midday; as it's the hinge to the rest of your day!

4. How you arrive home... It would be a shame to arrive to our work, school, and team... better than we arrive to our spouse and our children; or if you're single... to your own personal life! Choosing to enter your home and space with a smile and positive intent allows you to return home with love and/or self-love necessary for great relationships and habits; allowing you to truly enjoy the fruits of your labor!

5. Before Bed… Everything you've done up to this point has been awesome and great for you. But, without this cherry on top… you run the risk of being "Busy" instead of "Better". At the end of every night ask yourself "What was my BIG Accomplishment of the Day?" This will allow you to end every day with purpose and pride; and wake daily with vigor to do it again!

Become consistent in "The 5 Points of Your Day" and see how the things you choose to listen to, the people you choose to speak with, how you enter home in a positive manner, and giving each day purpose compound over time as it evolves from something you're trying, to a habit, to a lifestyle! (you can take the weekends off!)

> *"You chose your university, you chose your job, to start your business, be in that relationship, have that family…. then remember to act like it… and win the day!"*
> **– Andre Young**

CHAPTER 19

A Leader's Pacification: The Problem & The Solution

There is an ebb and flow to everything... including our work, our relationships, household, and our lives. There are times when we're strict and intensely focused on achieving the dream and fulfilling the processes that will get us there... and there're times we slack off, let things go, and chill. This is human nature and the more we can... and are willing to manage the ebb and flow of this will make us true leaders at work and in our personal lives!

In order to do this, the two most important things we must acknowledge and understand are... 1) What's done in the beginning, will be expected in the middle and the end. 2) Pacification rarely leads to success.

Years ago, I worked as a Mental Health Therapist in Alternative Schools and loved the job. What an awesome hands-on (sometimes, literally hands-on) way to make to make a positive impact in the lives of others, their families, and futures! As I watched many teachers come and go; I recognized one truth… The teacher that started the year soft and pacified students were very soon eaten alive and left to become dejected, frustrated, easily burnt-out, and lost the year! This was true EVERY TIME… and I never witnessed a teacher change the flow mid-year. If they were up for it… the beginning of the next school year was their shot!

This hard-to-watch-crash-and-burn truth wasn't due to their lack of knowledge, a lack of passion, or lack of effort; rather it was the presence of pacification and the absence of expectations. Most people are willing to do what they were initially trained, expected, and allowed to do. People, employees, students, and, our children… want to do what they've been doing… because it's familiar and a habit. If we start soft, with no expectations, and pacifying situations due to fear of being the "Bad Guy", their temper tantrums, or our anxiety… they will, by habit and nature, expect things to continue that way.

What do I mean by pacify? Watch a baby become uncomfortable and burst into crying… What do the parents do? They pick up the child and get the pacifier. They will tear their house apart searching for that pacifier, get in the car to go buy a new pacifier, get pacifiers ordered to their door in bulk… just to stop this little itty-bitty baby from crying! It's easy for us as people and new leaders to do the same. Instead we pacify our employees, our friends, children, our partners; allowing them to run rampant in our lives, the job, the classroom, and in our relationship without expectations and boundaries. Then… WE get frustrated, burnt-out, mad, then self-righteous as we feel justified to either do less and be less in the relationships… or explode with blame, accusations, and self-righteousness. This is what the typical process looks like: •

The supervisor who pacifies employees only to disappear into their office or is perpetually aggravated and stressed as all of the pressure falls onto them.

The husband or wife that has taken on all of the household duties and is now shut down emotionally or fuming all the time; making it impossible to evolve the relationship.

The parent that pacifies their children so they don't have to deal with temper-tantrums later feeling hopeless, broken, and a victim in their home or blames the children for their behavior bringing them to countless therapists asking for their kids to be "fixed".

The employee, spouse, and children aren't broken… your process is and if you're up for it… it will take work to fix it!

This is important to know… things don't have to stay this way! If you're a brand-new leader… this process will be easier. If you are in the midst of a mess, it WILL get harder before it gets better; as it's difficult, but not impossible to break habits. Some employees, students, partners, and kids are dying for the change because they see how dysfunctional things are. But remember, although they want to see the change… they want it for "the others" not so much when change and new expectation hit their doorstep.

Change is hard and at the least is anxiety-producing. There will be resisters and not everyone will end this journey of the Pacification Evolution with you… and as a leader, that's going to have to be ok! The trick is… to anticipate this and be ready for it. So, how to do it?

1. Know your vision: What you would like to accomplish, what's the destination, why it's important to you, why it's best for them, and what would they like to get from the experience… allowing us, as leaders to add value to the vision and more reason for them to follow and enhance their leadership skills!

2. Now that the vision is clear… EXPECTATIONS are a must! A vision without expectations is simply hope. Expectations set the groundwork for developing a process… what are WE going to do consistently to make our dream and vision come to fruition?

3. Expectations without consequences are merely suggestions. This is difficult for new leaders and people in general. It's easy to have a dream, it's easy to say how we get there, it can be a lot to hold people accountable. However, it's easier when we

have the buy-in, the word, and the commitment of others from the beginning. When behaviors stop matching the agreed-upon vision; it's now easier to confront, discuss, and get back on track. Consequences can be as small as a company's verbal warning or write-up, talking to that student after class or a detention, taking away the "All-Powerful Cell Phone" from your kid for the evening, communicating (not chastising) with your partner… or… as big as making that "Landmark Firing" of an employee, that suspension or expulsion of that student, disciplining our child, or that life-changing break-up with that partner; making things temporarily harder on us but forever learned for them! No matter what direction you choose… choose one; as people are watching and once the tide swings to apathy or they realize your words are just words; it's much harder to lead and steer the ship!

4. If dysfunction has already set in… I'd suggest the same, but before Step #1 of sharing the vision; be sure to accept FULL responsibility for the dysfunction. We are the leader and it's our fault. Express that things need, must, and will change, you hope they are with you, and in the face of change not everyone will finish the journey with you or the team.

Also, share that it's reasonable they may not believe change and evolution is coming (because it hasn't been the pattern) and they are welcome to speak with you about their role in the change, but not the role of others. Now, you are ready for Steps 1-3!

In an intimate relationship; be sure to acknowledge the relationship is not where it could be… not "should be", but "could be"! Share the positives of the relationship, followed by what you'd like to add, what they'd like to add, how to combine the two visions, and what you are willing to do. Lastly, thank them for making the conversation easier and being willing to dream with you!

Pacification will not only punish us; but also, those we're leading, the organization, and our lives. It's up to us as Leaders to be mindful of what we start, how we start, and how we continue!

"A vision without expectations is simply hope. Expectations without consequences are merely suggestions."
— Andre Young

WAY TO LEAD 4

DAILY LEADERSHIP

CHAPTER 20
G. R. E. A. T. Leadership

G REATNESS… what a word! It represents the pinnacle and triumph of our efforts to achieve our dream! To be revered for achieving, overcoming, and our continuous grind to excel. As a Pittsburg Steelers fan, I remember my team winning the Superbowl and their star receiver making several big plays at the end to win the game. He was later videoed on the sideline continuously yelling, "That's how you be great!". The truth is, we all have greatness in us… some of us are ready to let it out, win our definition of "Superbowls", and scream it from the rooftops; while others are nervous, scared to fail… or scared to succeed, don't know how or where to start, or have an unrealistic vision of what greatness is for themselves… wanting to live someone else's vision of "greatness". If you're ready and willing… Let's Get G. R. E. A. T.!

G—Glow

The first thing you must do is get the glow! What? In the 1980's there was a movie called "The Last Dragon"… I know, "cheesy", but still a classic! In the movie, once the Kung Fu Master mastered his craft, he earned a glow around his body and everyone knew his power. Have you ever seen someone enter a room; you didn't know who they were, but you knew they were somebody and someone you wanted and needed to meet? That's the Glow!

We achieve that Glow by being willing to perfect our craft; building our confidence, not our arrogance… exuding we are comfortable in who we are, what we can provide, and maintaining a positive attitude in all days… not just the "good" ones! Whether you are the custodian, the CEO, middle management, a parent, partner… dedicate yourself to being the best, dedicate time to learn more than you need to, dedicate time to learn what others need and deliver it, and smile while doing it… This tops off your glow! Remember… without daily effort the Glow cannot maintain and becomes more potential based… and potential does not equal greatness. Greatness is consistent… There will be ups and downs; as life is a rollercoaster and we are all human beings, but be consistent in how you choose to arrive, how you attempt, and your efforts to enjoy and overcome!

R—Respect

Have you ever wanted to meet your favorite celebrity, only to find out or be told how rude, disrespectful, or arrogant they are? How's that feel… Disappointing right? It doesn't take away from their awesome ability, but it sure doesn't complete the circle for you! Respect simply means you are treating the people around you: your co-workers, employees, employers, teammates, partner, and family with honor, effort, and respect for who they are as people. Yes, some people will make it harder than you'd like it to be… but Respect doesn't mean you have to date them! It means… you recognize them as a full person, with a life that exists as a person, partner, parent, and more. It means you do your best to understand and respect their "Why" allowing more empathy and allowing YOU to simply smile, use your manners of "please", "thank you", and hope you have a "great day"!

E—Expectations for Ourselves

In my book, 7 Ways to Love, I share how most of us are quick to marry and make vows to another person and relationship before ever thinking of making vows to ourselves. To be great and a leader, we must first make some vows to US and set some expectations for ourselves and our lives. These expectations may change over time as we change and evolve, but having an expectation sets a standard to maintain, strive for, and also works to weed out the negative people or things in our path. Hopefully, your company, team, or school have standards and expectations... if they don't or they are too low and you desire to be great... I'd start asking myself what you're doing there and what's your plan to EVOLVE?

A—Accept Challenges

No one or anything stays the same for long. After a while, we are either getting better or getting worse; or at the least... we're changing. Accepting challenges keeps us fresh, thinking, motivated, inspired, curious, and can set new expectations we never thought was in our realm. This is not to be confused with accepting every or any challenge... rather, the challenges accepted need to be on your desired path to greatness that stretches you a bit out of your comfort zone!

When I first started my business, I made tons of personal growth, relationship growth, and lifestyle enhancement videos. I enjoyed the process and still do... I love how I feel and think after doing a video; as it's difficult to consistently say positive and powerful things and not live them! However, in meeting with a consultant, he strongly suggested I start writing. At the time, I just developed my website and without written content there would be limited SEOs and other stuff I had no concept of.

To say it lightly, I was tremendously against writing! I had spent over 15 years, at that point in my life, as a Mental Health Therapist and didn't want any more paperwork EVER AGAIN!!! But... he strongly suggested I write three times per week and post it on my site. So, very reluctantly I did. So reluctantly… my first blog… I set a timer to see how long the damage would take. To my surprise… it took about 25 mins. I had no frame of reference if that was good or bad, but I knew I could sacrifice it. Five books later… I love it, can't stop, and wouldn't stop! Who knew! This challenge was aligned with my vision for impact, I accepted it, and Boom! Writing may not be the challenge you decide to accept… but something is… So, stay open!

T—Taint the Water

Simply said… Greatness taints the water! When a true leader enters the picture, the room, the organization, or the family… you feel it, can't deny it, and things are different. Greatness in leadership makes positive change, sets new expectations, and is ready for more! There will be growing pains; as everyone doesn't want to be great, not willing to change, or pay the toll of greatness. That's ok, because greatness already knew that!

There will be people professionally and personally that are ready right now… awesome! There are others on the fence… Good! And there will be the negative Nancys and Nicks… Noted! My Leader's 7 (coming later in this book); emphasizes learning the 7 Languages people want, need, and benefit most from hearing from their leaders will help; making it easier to understand, connect, and motivate. But… the most important thing to remember here is… Make an impact in the people who are ready! It's difficult to do it for EVERYONE. Timing is everything in people's lives. It is your job to still exist and be great when the non-ready get ready so they know where to go! Taint the water at your job, in your home, in your relationships and be G. R. E. A. T. today and every day!

> *"As a leader, it's your job to still exist and be great when the non-ready get ready so they know where to go, how to get there, and what to do!"*
>
> **– Andre Young**

CHAPTER 21

Make'em Feel Good

H ave you ever revisited your old job or school… how were you greeted? Have you ever witnessed an old employee return to a job… how were they greeted? What was the aura of the experience? Joy, smiles, hugs, and more are ready to welcome you once you understand the Platinum Rule of "Make'em Feel Good!" ? In this world… as in your relationships… you tend to get out of something what you put into something!

Most people are droning about their lives and their day… focusing on the Have-To's of work and family life. Most people will gravitate to the negative; complaining about the day, the weather, their jobs, and if you choose to listen long enough… their relationships. YOU get to be the one that's different and provide a new vision of hope into the environment, the workspace, their life, and yours! Sounds like a huge task? However, it's simpler than you think and only takes a bit of daily dedication.

The first thing to do is... SMILE. Sounds simple, but not many people do it; especially on Mondays, at work, as the average person trying to make it through just another week.

Second, be and remain positive. There will be hundreds of things to complain about if you wish... and people and life will test you! Be positive in your speaking and conversation. Focus on the positives; as well as the positives of change. If there is nothing positive to say or you are in a "mood" of your own... it's best to say nothing. Remove yourself from negative conversations... simply excuse yourself and state you have to take care of something... anything... somewhere else. If you're a braver soul... challenge the negative statements of others with an alternate perspective. For example, a co-worker begins to complain about protocol changes and putting down the boss, the job, the change. Perhaps you acknowledge that change is always happening and he/she (the boss) may not like it either, but has to do their job and part of their job is telling us. Or, "It's a tough spot for them to be in and I'm glad I don't have to deal with it". And that's it... you do not have to go back and forth!

You've made a valuable point... the miserable will continue to be miserable; while the level-headed can see value in your statement and move forward. It's important to note: when you do have a gripe... gripe to someone who can help you; not just to share with anyone and everyone who will listen! A one-to-one respectful and forward-focused conversation with the person who can make a difference will go much further than seeking out "Bobbleheads" to tell you how right you are and later make you look like a painful cog in the system.

Third, and most importantly, make people feel great about who they are and their dreams. To know who they are and what their dreams are... means you have to care enough to ask. How did they get to working the job they're in? What would they like to do in the future? What's their passion; if it's not the job they're working? What do they do for fun outside of the role you know them in? Make sure they know you genuinely think their dream and passion are awesome and they can achieve everything they mentioned. The most powerful statement I was ever challenged with was, "Why Not?".

Have fun and enjoy your time with the people you meet, work with, etc. Be sure to ask about and discuss their passions and dreams. Not many people in life fully believe their passion and dream are possible and YOU may be the only one that asks, questions, and promotes it in their life. Whether this relationship maintains over time or not... you will never be forgotten for how you made them feel and you never know when your paths will cross again. Make a mark in the lives of others and witness the circle of greatness that will begin to surround you!

The more deposits you make in their lives stemming from your interest, care, and respect for others... the stronger your relationships will be as a leader; making difficult conversations less frequent, less offensive and less sharp. The difficult conversations are those TALKS about unmet needs, disappointment, or sharing some hard observations with someone you value or care about... on the job or in your personal life. Those conversations are never easy... but remember... if you've made enough deposits... a few withdrawals won't bankrupt the relationship. Yes, it still matters how you say it... frequent deposits do not give a leader the green light to spout whatever they want and however they want.

What are the dreams of your Employees, Leaders, Players, Students, Partner, Kids, Parents, etc.? How can will you help them achieve it?

CHAPTER 22

T. R. B. ing to Leadership

B ack in the day, before we were able to use our phones to hit a few buttons for pin-point accurate directions to get anywhere on the planet... we had to use this thing called a map. They were neatly folded in the glove compartment of your car and when unfolded it would take up the entire front windshield of the car; talk about distracted driving! However, the idea of the map is a wonderful thing and easily showed there was more than one way to get anywhere. Some roads would take you directly to your destination... while others would provide a longer but more scenic route. Through You Evolving Now and my speaking engagements, I have several formulas to achieve success and help people become better leaders in their 4 P's; and people sometimes ask, "Why do you have more than one?"... and I respond, "Because they all work!". Just like a map, the concepts of my 7 Ways to Lead will get you to your destination of leadership; some concepts may be more direct, some more scenic, some fit your current personality, while others are a glimpse of the personality you desire. T.R.B. is a simple, but powerful formula I learned many years ago as a leader and I look forward to it impacting you!

T—Trust

Trust is a special word and for some… trust may be difficult to give; allowing the people in your vision of success the necessary space to grow and evolve. For others, trust is too easily given; allowing people to run amuck with a plethora of ideas that don't align with your vision and desired path. What I learned was… Trust is not Blind. As a leader you must be willing to inspect what you expect and also be willing to teach!

Years ago, I was in charge of a team and later inherited new team members as time went on. One member of the team was a seasoned woman, strong in her field and passionate about her work. Another was a newly hired male staff, eager to assist, and everyone turned to for assistance. The two were paired to run a group for struggling teens. This was a no-brainer! This pairing couldn't fail if they tried… right? Well, due to this thinking, I admit… I neglected to attend their group for months as I was sure they had everything under control. How could they not? Until one day, things were a bit slow, I poured a cup of coffee and entered the group to observe and engage. I was applauded!!! The new male team member dominated conversation, told stories of his famed sports past, talked over the seasoned new team member, and shot down points she made in front of the group. She appeared visibly frustrated, the teens were visibly getting nothing out of the experience, and the woman team member didn't share her frustrations with me. Wow! I immediately accepted full responsibility, apologized one-on-one to each team member, and began my new and EVOLVED definition of trust!

As leaders, it's imperative we trust people to be how they ARE… not how we want them to be, how we believe they can be, or how we believe they should be. Trust them to be how they present themselves and how they operate in good times, bad times, and steady times. Most people aren't lying to us… However, we seem to think, want, or believe they will be different when we want them to be... and in the case of my story above... I did a poor job of teaching how to effectively run a group session, how to start, what the middle needs to consist of, best ways to close, and best follow-up practices; allowing for a collaboration of ideas. We must be willing to teach HOW things work, why they work, and allow for creativity along the way. It's easy to get so busy being busy... we quickly spout off words, acronyms, and procedures that are old to us... but may be new, different, and confusing to them; completely ignoring the concept of different learning styles.

We must also be willing to *set expectations*. This can be difficult, as you don't want to sound like a "Boss"! But, what's the alternative? Be Mindful to set expectations for impact, expectations for respect, professionalism, and for whatever is in line with your vision and mission! In this scenario, I would have benefited from setting an expectation that this is a professional facility; focused on respect and impacting others with quality organized groups that will be monitored and reviewed weekly. As a leader, I didn't do my part and they eventually did things their way and clashed when expected to work together; ultimately hurting the consumer, the reputation of the organization, and my reputation as a leader.

R—Respect

In order to enhance trust, we must be willing to understand and respect another person's superpower; what they bring of value and how that value will benefit the team, the vision, and the mission. This will also include putting them in the right seat to succeed. Many new leaders, as I did, wanted everyone to have their superpower. Let's put our people in their natural position; allowing them to enjoy their successes and witness their value in the Bigger Picture!

A second "R" here would be to Reward. There are many different ways to reward. Remember, behavior that gets ignored tends to get repeated... But also... behavior that gets rewarded tends to get repeated... Be Mindful!

B—Build

Be conscious of the language you choose. Is it positive, optimistic, powerful, motivating, inspiring, and uplifting? Most people don't expect raises, the big promotion, or in sports to be the captain... but all of these individuals can benefit from being "built-up". The significance of Construction Talk is two-fold. When we choose to speak nicely, encouraging, and positively to another person it does something powerful to them; making them feel noticed, valued, and special. It also does something for us and our mission... when we apply construction talk, not only in front of the person... but away from their presence; as you're speaking to other people... it keeps you positive, inspired, and appreciative ourselves; and it sure doesn't hurt when great news like that gets back to that person and your team!

"It's easy to get so busy being busy... we quickly spout off words, acronyms, and procedures that are old to us... but may be new, different, and confusing to them; Be Mindful"
– Andre Young

CHAPTER 23

Ride That Rollercoaster

"Ohhhhh Shooooot!" is what I used to scream when I rode rollercoasters; taking that slow ride all the way up, seeing the people on the ground as small as ants, then slowly falling over the crest into warp speed! Notice, I said used to ride rollercoasters! When you're younger the dips, turns, twists, speed, and height don't affect you as much. However, with age comes some limitations... or at least an unwillingness to voluntarily put your body, mind, and spirit through such an ordeal.

Some people love rollercoasters, can't get enough, and are one with the motion of going with the flow. While others, prefer the security and control of being on solid ground, limited risk, and relaxing in safe confines. However, there are no safe confines in the world of leadership and rollercoasters are a lot like life, leadership, and success. It may start off slow and you can't wait for it to pick up... so you can feel the adulation of your success, making your own decisions, making your own path and mark. This success doesn't come stress or worry-free; as many leaders express concern and anxiety in making hard but necessary change, managing many people, managing old friends, managing people older or more experienced than themselves, or people they don't necessarily care for or respect (we don't always get to lead who we like and respect). It's easy for the Success Thieves named fear and self-doubt... or... on the opposite end... our "ego" to step in; whispering destructive things into our head. Then... POW... off you go at warp speed with all the highs, lows, twists, and turns of leadership and success!

The way to EVOLVE and master the rollercoaster of success and leadership is to maximize the highs, minimize the lows, don't let the twists and turns take your eyes off the vision and mission, and pull into the station at the end, wide-eyed, knowing you've just lived and conquered!

Maximizing your highpoints means you recognize and celebrate your successes, the success of your team, and its individual members both big and small. It's easy to glaze over achieved deadlines and accomplishments living at mock-speed from duty to duty, deadline to deadline, and focusing on some distant goal you think will mean success... only to really mean... more work and raised expectations. YOU are a success NOW. Allow yourself and your team to benefit now, celebrate now, and enjoy the victories! Enjoy them for as long as you can, prepare for growth and new tasks, and remember to pull you and your team into the station from time-to-time to rest, reset, and enjoy!

Minimizing your lows does not mean you trivialize your low points or minimize the low points of others. There is value in all feelings. Sadness, hurt, frustration, anger, etc. and are not to be undervalued and can have a tremendous impact on your success and leadership... but we cannot live there! Acknowledge your feelings and the feelings of others, understand why you or they are thinking and feeling that way, build a team of supporters, and work to build/rebuild/and fortify within the rules and mission of your structure. Or, as a leader, modify and create new useful rules and guidelines that make sense... common sense... for you, your team, your people, and life! It's called… being a Leader! Hard Times are awful for everyone, no one is exempt, and some scars never fully heal; but they all can teach and will make us either bitter or better.

Lastly, everyone will eventually pull into the station; whether it's termination, downsizing, retirement, or death. You will have an end… everyone will (sorry to be morbid!). For some, its 20 years from now… for others, it may be tomorrow. Make sure you pull into the station, wide-eyed and knowing you lived a heck of a life and helped lead people to live their best!

> *"Hard Times are awful for everyone, no one is exempt, and some scars never fully heal; but they all can teach and will make us either bitter or better."*
>
> **– Andre Young**

CHAPTER 24

Enhancing Our "Middle Strength"

As a leader, you have an interest, a goal, a dream... Great for you! The beginning of anything, although nerve-racking, can be a fun time! It's a time of possibility, vision, ideas, and immediate gratification of things coming into existence that were not there yesterday! Conversely, the end of something can be sad, heart-wrenching, but rewarding; as you recap all you have built, learned, and can pass on. But, as a leader... what about the middle?

Whether your interest, dream, or goal is your job, a relationship, or other personal endeavors... The middle is where real life happens! The middle is where we find out who you really are, what you're really made of, and provides all the opportunities you'll need to make it to success with pride! I learned this all too much as a college football player and this lesson continues to inspire me throughout every day of my life and hopefully yours. During the beginning of the season... you have a vision of success, your goals, and excitement for the opportunity to be great and leave your mark. You train daily, go to camp, go through the grind, and the season begins! You make it through a few games and BAM! You hit the wall... you hit a point where the grind has become monotonous, you begin to lose interest, lose focus, just wanting to get through it, and an average mindset begins to take over with constant complaining about things you were so excited for just a few short months ago.

But fear not... the end of any season is always near... now it's time to pick it up again and make a dash for something meaningful to salvage the season, your pride, attain those goals you laxed on, and prove you are better than an average win-loss record. Sounds a lot like life, huh? Most people go through this same process at their job, in their relationships, and in their lives... only with much higher stakes at risk than a good win-to-loss ratio. The biggest loss is droning through an average existence at work, in relationships, and in life; knowing you had more to offer and the ability to lead your life and the people in it! The EVOLVED individuals and teams learn how to minimize this slump and most importantly... how to maximize what I call "Middle Strength"; allowing them the opportunity to fight, lead, and finish strong!

"Middle Strength" is your ability to stay focused and willing while DOING your company's mission, the vows you spoke at the altar, the oath you made to your team or family on a daily basis.... even on the days YOU don't feel like it. "Middle Strength" involves YOU remaining organized, effectively managing your time, taking care of yourself; knowing when rest is necessary, when to uplift others, being an intentional learner, and possessing the ability to proactively adjust... even when... especially when you don't want to! The new regime of employees, students, recruits, and leaders are coming... and when they get there... what kind of leader will they find?

As a leader, what do you need to Stop Doing, Start Doing, and Continuing Doing to best impact your Middle Strength?

CHAPTER 25
Clear & Concise Leadership

H ere are a few scenarios to explore. Have you ever received instruction from someone and did what they asked, only to be told how bad a job you did? Leaving you feeling bewildered and not good enough? Have you ever received instruction; only to be left feeling confused, but too nervous to ask for clarity... thinking it must be you and you'll do your best to figure it out? Or, have you received zero instruction; handled the situation to the best of your ability, knowledge, and capacity... only to be told how you handled it was wrong? I can go on, but you get the point!

Much of this can be avoided with enhanced Clear & Concise Leadership! Of course, no one can cover or prepare for every event and we must be willing to let our people improvise and problem-solve; but leadership requires anticipation. As leaders, let's be able to anticipate as many situations as possible and provide clear and concise plans for action. Whether in a business, school, or in our family… what are your expectations? What are the rules? What are the consequences? What are the plans for important and anticipated scenarios?

- Are the expectations, rules, consequences, and plans clear to everyone. Are they simple enough and easy enough for everyone to understand?
- A simpler, but necessary question then becomes… Is everyone aware?

Clear & Concise Leadership is also two-fold! As a Leader, it's our job to ensure answers to the questions listed above. It's also our job to take various learning styles into consideration. One day, I asked my awesome wife to help me with a computer issue I was having in my office. My wife is a Bam-Bam get it done personality, speaks fast, and is then quickly off to the next thing. As she stood over my shoulder rattling off words, explanations, and directions… My head was spinning! She then took over my keyboard and began to do the process for me. Although, my problem was solved quicker; there was no way EVER was I going to be able to repeat the process or do it on my own. This situation plays out in many businesses, trainings, schools, and families. The leader is knowledgeable, means well, and can fix the problem… but can unknowingly create a frustrating system where they maintain team or individual incompetence and become frustrated that they are continually the "Fixer" of everyone's' problems!

My wife is amazing and her capacity to learn is very different from mine… she was simply teaching me the way that she learns best. However, I'm a very hands-on learner and need a walkthrough once or twice. I'm also a bit ADD (Attention Deficit Disorder) and have learned how to be successful in spite of it; but struggle to learn things I don't care about or don't often do. Over the years I have learned to keep a notebook and use it to write down the process of things I don't do often; allowing me to refer to my book and not to people. A huge headache-saver for me... and other people! My point is... as Leaders, realize everyone doesn't have the same learning style as you. Make your points clear and concise and be as sure as you can that people understand and have the freedom to ask questions.

As the person receiving the information... be aware of your learning style and how your leaders can best impart great knowledge and skills to you. Looking back and understanding what I know now, I regret my effort level as a college football player. Although, I played a lot throughout my years... I didn't become a full-time starter until my senior year. As a non-starter you get limited repetitions during practice to get familiar with the plays and adjustments for the upcoming game. As a professional back-up athlete... you may get none. Taking notes after practice, making, and creating time to walk through the plays on my own or with other back-ups after practice would have paid dividends! You can't go back... but you can always do your best to become a better learner; not putting it all on your leaders to fix your deficiencies. Greatness is a choice... and a process! Choosing to do this is personal leadership and a valuable part of leadership!

As a leader, on a scale of 1-10, how do you rate your communication skills... as a Professional? A Parent? A Partner? How will you move up 1 or 2 spots in each? As a learner, how do you rate your ability to accept, understand, and apply new information; especially the information you don't like or care about? What will you do to move up 1 or 2 spots?

"Greatness is a choice... and a process!"
– Andre Young

CHAPTER 26

Lead with H. E. A. T.

M ost people can give orders, but not everyone can be a leader! When you lead... be mindful to lead with H.E.A.T. and allow evolution to take its course! So, how do you do it?

H—Humble

Remember, you didn't make it this far all by yourself. There have been many who have crossed your path, both positive and negative; offering learning experiences to make you the YOU of today and tomorrow. Stay humble and remain dedicated to your ability to positively impact the lives of others... not living off of the validation of your title. Jobs and titles can easily come and go... but you'll have YOU and your reputation forever. Remember what it was like to go through the grind of entry-level work, the squeeze of middle management, to be new to a position and have to figure things out on the fly at warp-speed; while trying to figure out all the personalities around you... it will help your ability to remain humble as a leader!

E—Excitement

Be excited about the life you get to live! No one wants to follow a leader who complains and hates their life, their job, and their relationship... I've worked for them and it takes all of your personal leadership to manage that ordeal; as I once had a supervisor tell me I was too positive!

If you don't currently like your life... change it! If you can't, find the positives and work to change YOU! As you go... your team will go... so be excited about the journey. Realize things will change, as nothing can ever stay the same forever. So, find the positives in the change, focus on the bigger picture while paying respect to the pain and struggle of the little picture, and help your team to move forward; taking in their needs, wants, and helpful insights! Negativity is like quicksand and will swallow you and your team whole if you stand still... move on, move forward, and with a positive attitude!

A—Anticipate

You are a leader... you must anticipate the peaks, valleys, storms, positives, and negatives of situations. Stay ahead of your curve by setting time to EVOLVE. You can do this by intentionally reading, learning, and being inquisitive about your craft, business, team members, family, etc. I'm a father of four and a leader in my home (Not THE leader, but certainly a leader). The power of being able to anticipate made the transition into the adolescence phase of my children much easier for me (Not easy... but easier!).

As my first child turned 12, I thought she actually lost her mind. It was if she went upstairs one night and an alien abducted my daughter, but left behind a much meaner clone. A clone that had a mouth and used it to always have the last word... What the heck! But, by the second go-round... I was much more prepared and anticipated the behaviors, attitude, need for privacy, and all that comes with the dreaded... but now better understood teen-age years!

As a leader, you may have found that your employees, students, athletes usually interview well... or else you wouldn't have brought them into the organization. They usually perform great when their job is on the line, but what do you and can you anticipate in the middle? Perhaps, some employees and players will lax in the middle of projects, are going to become overwhelmed with so much new information, or are going to become grouches without vacation time over a long period of time, or may be looking for a new beginning after a certain amount of years. Be mindful of the flow, knowing what to expect, and take pride in being able to anticipate the needs and wants of your team. Be a leader that is proactive instead of stuck in reactive mode; as it's hard to move forward when you are always cleaning up messes!

T—Tough Teaching

There are times as a leader when you must have that tough conversation, say the tough thing, make that tough decision, and teach that tough lesson. Do not hesitate... most people know when they are wrong or insufficient in an area and expect the tough talk to happen. When it doesn't... YOU have given permission for it to continue. Do it now, do it respectfully, be clear, concise, and be sure to get clarification that the new expectations are understood... Your leadership and their growth is counting on it!

> *"Negativity is like quicksand and will swallow you and your team whole if you stand still... move on, move forward, and move with a positive attitude!"*
>
> **– Andre Young**

CHAPTER 27

Right-Seat Leadership

As a leader, there are many seats you get to lead, manage, and mold. Every seat represents a person, someone's position or title, and a talent that wields their own superpower; making them a special asset to the team! Not all, but many new leaders make the common mistake of attempting to direct with their ego. Most are good men and women and don't mean to or do so with malice; rather they believe their way is best because that's the way they achieved success. Or, the Newly Appointed Leader wants everyone to have, know, and learn their superpower because it's what got THEM there. They want everyone to care as much as they do, give as much as they do, sacrifice as much as they did and do, and treat their definition of success as if it was their baby too. Well... it's not their baby, your people have their own superpower, and are entitled to not work at your break-neck, non-stop, diabolical pace!

This leads me to one of my first and most memorable mistakes as a new leader! Many years ago, I was appointed to leadership to supervise a team of four awesome individuals. I was a supervisor of a Mental Health Team at a Center-Based Partial Hospitalization Alternative School. My specialty was Individual and Group Therapy. My superpower was connecting with clients, teachers, parents, and administration very easily; making me an asset in the world of crisis management… and I don't mean missing a business deadline type of crisis… rather physical harm and suicidal crisis! I wanted my team to excel therapeutically; as I valued that particular attribute due to my recent completion of my Master's Degree.

However, looking back… my team consisted of a 6ft 5in 350lb man that was awesome at connecting, great at crisis intervention, and preferred to be in the classroom setting. A woman that was detailed oriented, way more organized than I, and great at free-time activities. Another woman that knew every student's bio, was not strong at connecting or counseling, but awesome at interagency networking and always had an answer to a question. The problem was… I was focused on creating "Mini-Me's"; I was "ego-blind" to the awesome team in front of me that could have been way more productive efficient, happier, and most importantly benefited the organization, the students, and their families had I focused on their superpowers and created a system that allowed them to use them.

I had the best Crisis Manager, the best Activity Coordinator, and the best Case-Manager sitting right in front of me… and I failed to maximize their superpower, allowing them to fully enjoy their time at work, their calling, and their job. Leadership involves US being willing to put our people in the right seat to cultivate and maximize their superpower and evolve the system that already exists. Be sure to teach your superpower also; as you have a gift they can incorporate into their toolbox and create an environment where people want to come because they feel honored to get to do what they're great at!

Right-Seat Leadership may also require us to be flexible and get creative! I hate boxes. "Hate" is a strong word, but I do hate boxes! Yes, boxes are useful and necessary and I understand they provide clear lines, divisions of labor, and rules. I often joke with my wife that I didn't want to be in a box in life so when I die don't put me in a box in the ground! As leaders, we can become very "box-driven" and everything, including our people, team, kids, etc. need to fit neatly in boxes to satisfy us, or the numbers, or protocol. Yuck!

I once worked in sales and saw a woman enter the store. The way she entered, how she carried herself, and how she engaged with others... I swore she was upper management. Come to find out, she was interviewing for an entry-level position at the store. She was hired, but not for the entry-level position... rather for a newly created position just for her to impact the store, the employees, and the customers with her energy, guidance, and support. Freak'in WOW!!!!

Due to my position at the time, I'm not sure how things continued behind the scenes for the woman or the company... but WOW! I fell in deep respect for a company and leadership that took Right-Seat Leadership to the next level and was willing to create a seat that didn't exist for a superpower they noticed and were willing to cultivate. Be mindful to let your superpower shine so bright it can't be ignored and your company or team doesn't want to be without it! Be mindful to appreciate, cultivate, and reward the superpowers of those following your lead... as a compliment for who they are and what they bring to the table!

A Few Right-Seat Leadership Questions:

- *What are the superpowers of the people on your team: at work, school, in your home, your partner?*
- *How will you appreciate, cultivate, and encourage their superpowers and efforts moving forward?*
- *Are your people in the right-seat at your job, on your team, and/or in your home?*
- *Is there a new seat you can create for an awesome talent at your job, on your team, and/or in your home?*

"A leader's duty is to impart wisdom, enhance skill sets, promote forward-thinking, and identify and value of your peoples' superpowers… cultivating them and helping them to excel past the point of which they believed they could go! During this process it's also imperative to put butts in the right seats."

– Andre Young

CHAPTER 28

A Leader's Question

Although I have a Master's Degree... school and I did not get along for many years! I think back to school and sitting in rows, forced memorizing, receiving lower grades based on the correct APA Style instead of my content, and many other irritations that still frustrate me to this day! I ended my 10th-grade year with a stellar 4 F's, two D's, and a C. I can still remember my mother's face as she squinted trying to comprehend the letter "F" on my report card... and four of them to boot! I struggled to understand why my grades were so low; as I went to school and attended classes daily... but something was off.

Thankfully my passion for football was a driving and motivating force for me to show up to school and do what I had to do, so I could do what I wanted to do! Football enabled me to attend college and it wasn't until my Junior year I discovered how I learned best and how to study. It also helped that my classes became more interesting to me and more introspective as I selected Sociology as my major area of study.

In graduate school... all of my classes were introspective as I studied Counseling Psychology with a specialty in Marriage and Family Counseling. My grades soared and so did I. What I realized is... I had difficulty with attention and focus... and an even harder time learning things I didn't care about. I also benefited greatly from writing down tasks and referring back to it to embed it in my head. This also played out in sports; as I move up levels from high school to college, to professional... if you're not the starter; there are less and less reps (practice plays) for you. Being able to witness, simulate on your own, and write things down... can become your best friend in order to keep your job! But.... In all my years of schooling and playing... no teacher, coach, or employer ever asked me how I learned best!

As with my Leader's 7 (coming up later in the book), most leaders will speak the language they are most comfortable with to motivate their team, but what if your employees, team, partner, kids, etc. speak a different language? Most leaders will teach and train new employees and teammates in the language that's easiest to them, but how about this as a Leader's Question... *"How do you learn best?"* Of course, every organization has its own protocol and time constraints that must be respected... however, when we can and where we can... isn't this a powerful question?

Have you ever had someone explain something to you and you struggled to understand, keep up, only to become more and more anxious as the other person becomes noticeably more frustrated and not concerned with changing their style! Now... add a pending performance review on top of it (that happens in sports too). How cool would it be if that same person asked you, "How do you learn best?" and they mixed in their style with want you needed most! That's Leadership!

4 Styles of Learning

1. Visual—Teach the person via pictures or video
2. Auditory—Use sound or music to teach

3. Verbal—Teach utilizing words and/or writing
4. Physical—Teach by allowing the person to do. (A Hands-On Learner)

The power of The Leader's Question played out with my wife and I; as I explained earlier when I asked for her help with the issue on my computer. My wife is a tech genius… especially compared to me… and was more than willing to help. She stood over my shoulder and spit a barrage of words at me and I was lost! Then she assumed control of my keyboard and mouse to fix the problem. She was being her version of helpful… but I was left lost, frustrated, and no more knowledgeable than I was when I started. My question is… *Whose keyboard and mouse may you be grabbing as a Professional, a Partner, a Parent, etc.?*

I implore you to utilize the "Leader's Question" the next time you're struggling to understand why your employee, player, student, or child are simply "Not getting it". Remember, it could be several reasons you've never considered. It's your duty as a leader to care enough to ask and apply how another person learns best; enhancing their ability to EVOLVE!

A few other powerful Leader's Questions:

- What's your dream? Is there any way I can help you get there?
- How can I best help you?
- Why are you here and what do you want to get out of the experience of being here?

"It's your duty as a leader to care enough to ask the right questions and apply effective ways to impact how another person learns best; enhancing their ability to EVOLVE!"

– Andre Young

CHAPTER 29

A Leader's Attention

We all can be leaders... if we choose to be. A leader of your own life, in a professional position of leadership, as the custodian, or most importantly in how you choose to show up in your life as a Person, a Professional, Partner, and Parent! Choosing to act as a leader is not for the faint-of-heart; as it will come with its laundry list of responsibilities that can easily drain you and steal your attention from the things that will make your success worth having... I call them "Attention Drainers"!

Perhaps, it's that project at work with the deadline you must make in order prove your worth, move up in the company, get that bonus, or keep you in good standing... which will be one of thousands of deadlines that will be expected of you! I've had several companies push back meetings with me on beginning internal ways to enhance leadership and work/life harmony for their employees and team due to being project busy, deadlines, and not the right time. I certainly believe timing is important... however, is there ever a time when a project has stopped and there was nothing to do? In my experience, there are always multiple projects in the works, one waiting, and "Busy" is always ready to jump on our backs!

As a leader, be sure to meet your deadlines and dominate those projects; being mindful not to let your task become an "Attention Drainer"; leading you to ignore the needs and wants of your staff, your team, and your loved ones! We can only put people on hold for so long until they Burn-Out or Bore-Out... and are no longer the same or there at all when you are ready to return to them.

Perhaps your "Attention Drainer" is that awesome new life milestone... a new home, a baby, a wedding, etc.! If this is happening in your life right now... a BIG Congrats to you! However, it's always amazed me how such great milestones can also become "Attention Drainers". We become so consumed with planning the wedding, decorating our new home, or caring for the kids... we completely neglect our husband, wife, boyfriend, or girlfriend... our family and friends... only to look up one day and have achieved our singular definition of success, but not the relationships to go with it! A leader knows that success with no one to share it with is the saddest feeling in the world. So, what to do?

This is where I usually give you my two, three, or four-step plan on how to evolve leadership and work/life harmony. Today is different and a bit simpler... however, without your want-to, application, and consistency it won't work. Simply, the answer is to stay curious! In my last book, "7 Ways to Love" I shared curiosity didn't kill the cat... it saved the relationship. The same is true with our leadership! Stay curious about your employees at work and your loved ones outside of work.

When I had staff, I often asked what I call "The Get Great Question" and it sounded like this... "I love doing what we get to do and I'm happy to have you on the team; What do you want to get out of the experience working here? What do you like and what needs to be tweaked?". In my personal life, I ask a similar question to my wife from time to time... "I love you and I love us... I want to be a great husband to you; is there anything you need from me?".

This simple effort of curiosity allows you to stay connected with your people, allows you to know what's working... not just what you think is working, and allows you to digest what is an issue of concern. I often share this concept with leaders during my Seminars and Leadership Programs and stress three important points that are monumentally necessary for your curiosity to work:

1. Your people must TRUST that you and other leaders can accept answers and complaints that may be hard to hear. Have you worked consistently to develop a culture of positivity and trust? Scared employees, scared significant others, and scared kids don't want to share thoughts, feelings, wants, and needs they will be punished for later!

2. Your curiosity may not automatically get you the "real answer". Remember... you've been pondering the question, practicing the question in your head, and finally hit them with it. They have not been thinking of it and may not be ready to answer when you decide to ask. Think about it... an employee decides to use "The Get Great Question", stops their boss, and says "Hi boss, I want to be great here... can you help me? What do I have to do to be better?". This is a fair and great question... but perhaps the boss was on their way to the bathroom, to a meeting, has a million things on their mind swirling like a tornado, or may not trust the employee can handle hard-to-hear feedback... or the boss simply doesn't like confrontation. The boss may deflect; giving a half-hearted answer or the dreaded... "You're doing great; just keep it up!". As a leader, accept the fact you've caught a person off guard but do not accept a weak answer. Allow them time to gather their thoughts and articulate a leader's response. It may sound like this, "Thank you for saying I'm doing good, but I really do want to be the best and know how I can improve. Can we set up a time to talk? When would be best for you? This is how we help our leaders to lead us. This is how we help our

loved ones to teach us. Remember… don't ask the question if you can't handle the answer!

3. As a leader, once you know… you can't unknow… and to know and ignore is the very opposite of leadership! Is what your people or relationship need from you as a leader reasonable, doable, and fair? If so… great! Do it… and do it a bit past your comfort zone! If it's not reasonable, doable, or fair… explain why, share the bigger picture view and work to brainstorm ways to better meet the needs and concerns.

A Leader's Attention must be paid to the task at hand, but also to THE PEOPLE that make the task possible. The people at work that help make the deadline possible, the people at home supporting the long-hours and stress, and the people you're doing all that hard work for… your kids! The "Attention Drainers" are everywhere… won't stop and don't plan on stopping. Get curious about your people; learn and apply what is most needed to become the leader they need!

What do your employees or employer need from you most right now?
What does your relationship need most from you right now?
What do your children need most from you right now?

Your answers to these questions will allow for true Leadership and Work / Life Harmony! Enjoy!

CHAPTER 30

A Leader's Problem-Solving

I f you're interested in living the life of your dreams... professionally and personally... you must first choose to become a leader! The good this is, anyone and everyone can be a leader; depending on how we choose to show up.... Show up in our job, our relationships, our lives! Do you have a vision for yourself, your team, and your lifestyle? Are you positive, optimistic, ready, knowledgeable, willing, and consistent in good and hard times? If yes, great! If not, now you know the formula! As leaders, two things are inevitable; change and problems. I'd rather view problems as opportunities, but either way... problems/opportunities are coming! For leaders, professionally and personally, I have found it always seems to be a problem or two that's been long-standing and ignored that's currently poising professional culture or relationships in their life. Most people can play the role of leader and tolerate these problems when things are great or even OK, but what do you do when you're ready for change, ready to address it, and evolve?

Announcement

A leader must first be aware that a problem exists in order to be willing to address it. Without initial awareness and willingness, the dysfunction will continue and rarely gets better on its own. This next step, Announcement, is an important first step and many individuals sitting in positions of leadership forget it; becoming even more responsible for the dysfunction.

Once you are aware of the problem, it's impact, and are willing to address it... it's now time to ANNOUNCE the process of change! This announcement can be made 1-on-1 to people or in a group setting. Realize... your team at work: co-workers, employees, employers, etc. have been doing the dysfunction for a long time and for a very simple reason... because they can! The people in your personal life: significant other, kids, and family... have been behaving in a way that is unbecoming to you... because they can!

It starts with a leader accepting they have allowed dysfunction to occur and MUST accept full responsibility before taking another step. Yes, it would be great if the people on your team and in your life would do the same... but true leaders accept the hit and the process of moving forward. In a loss, the star coach or quarterback does not blame their team... they accept full responsibility in losses and none of the credit in the wins!

The announcement may sound like, "I understand _____ has been occurring and it's been this way for a while. As a leader here, I accept full responsibility for not addressing it. Things will be changing as we move forward. The new rule/standard/expectation is _____. I'm aware this may not be easy for everyone. My vision is _____ and I hope you will be a part of it.". In a professional or parental setting, it may be appropriate to explain expectations and consequences for lack of follow-through. In a personal setting, asking for a commitment and plan to work together as a team may be a more beneficial approach. The point is to share the new way, a new day, and be sure everyone is aware. It would be unfair to suddenly penalize someone for something they have always been allowed to do under your poor leadership. Set a new standard, make an announcement, and lead!

Boundary

As mentioned above, your team is depending on you to set boundaries, keep them, and enforce them. The biggest complaints I hear working with companies and leaders are:

1. Our leaders don't know how to lead
2. We are in a state of change and "Busy"

Two of the biggest complaints I hear from employees are:

1. "There are no consequences given to people who don't follow the rules.". The fact that employees are not receiving any consequences may be true or untrue. That uncooperative employee may be reprimanded behind closed doors as the company or team follows company policy. Not everything is every employee's business to know. The important thing to note is… your employees, teams, kids, and love-ones all know the rules, when they are broken, and what to expect! Why should anyone change if they continuously get to do what they want, how they want, and when they want. As a leader, boundaries are a necessary roadmap to get to your definition of success!
2. Lack of consistency

Consequences

What are the consequences for an employee coming in late, not following rules or standards, etc.? What are the consequences for your kids not doing the dishes or bringing home poor grades? If there is a hard and fast rule in place, are they aware? Is the consequence reasonable and fair for both you and them? Be mindful… many hard and fast rules don't always do justice in real-life situations. Also, can you actually DO the consequence... firing all staff and having no company to run typically is not the best business strategy. Parents, can you exist in your house with your kids with no Fortnite or technology for them to play for a month? Sounds funny, but it's the truth! Be sure the consequence fits both of you!

If the consequences can fluctuate and can be different for different people... be sure to be clear about it upfront. Jimmy Johnson, ex-Dallas Cowboys football coach, is a great example. He was upfront and said to his team that he cared about everyone, but everyone will not be treated equally. If a star player made a big mistake, there was one type of consequence. If a third-string player made the same mistake... he'd be cut! He also informed star-players before practice he was going to be extra hard on them on a particular day in efforts to motivate other players; explaining to the star... if they see me yelling at you; they know they have no chance to mess up... only enhancing the quality of the team! Fair or unfair... he announced it, set boundaries, and explained consequences... leading us into the last step!

Consistency

As a leader, professionally or personally, be sure to be consistent! Your people can deal with almost anything... as long as they know what to expect! Be consistent in your vision, your standard, your expectations, and how you show up each day! Have you ever engaged with someone that was different from day-to-day? They say "Hello" some days but not others? They give great effort one day and not others? They are present some days and absent others? Eventually, we tend to stop talking to these individuals, we expect nothing from them, and we eventually do things our own way because we can't count on them. That's how your team, your employees, and love-ones feel about you when your leadership is inconsistent.

Whatever problem you're facing or problem that will arise, evolve with these steps to become the leader you are meant to be. Here's a recap:

Announce—Become aware of what the problem is and best ways to solve it. Then announce a new day has come, you accept full responsibility, and set a new vision and standard!

Boundaries—These are expectations of how to do tasks and engage in relationships. Be sure the boundaries can actually be done by the people you are asking. If so, great! If not, what's a more reasonable way to begin collecting smaller wins?

Consequences—This is a leader's least favorite thing to do. Consequences sound like such an awful word and can become a potential abuse of power in the hand of a negative leader. But remember, a vision without expectations is just hope, and expectations without consequences are merely suggestions!

Consistent—Choose a way and do growth consistently; allowing evolution to take it's course as you move forward!

"A vision without expectations is just hope; expectations without consequences are merely suggestions"

– Andre Young

CHAPTER 31
A Leader's R. O. P. E.

Whether you're a person in a position of leadership or a leader in regards to how you choose to show up in your life, your job, and relationships (anyone can be a leader; depending on how you choose to show up, smile, do your best, and be your best)... every leader will have to make the decision of how much rope they are going to give their people. Some will give too much rope before individuals are ready; leading to employees or other people in their lives to run amuck with not enough experience or training to make positive and forward-thinking decisions. Some leaders will not give enough rope; stifling their people and either burning-them-out due to micromanaging or boring-them-out due to a minimal and unchallenging workload. So, how does a person in a position of leadership know how much rope to give and how does a leader get more rope given?

R—Respect Superpowers

I love superhero movies; the drama, the action, special effects, and of course… the superpowers! Each character has their own special ability, knows how to use it, control it, and is identified by it. These amazing individuals then form a super team and take on the world of adversity! Although the movies and characters are fictional; not much is different in real life. Every person on the planet possesses their own superpower! Some find it early and hone it, some find it late, while some never choose to expand it or see how strong their superpower can get or take them. The point is, everyone has one. Therefore, as a leader, everyone on your team has one and it's your job to see it, help hone it, utilize it for the good of the goal, and develop a team of diverse superpowers ready to accomplish a variety of tasks, projects, and take on all adversity!

Respecting Superpowers will give you more confidence in how much rope to give your people as well as what specific roles and tasks best match their power. In contrast, knowing your superpower will increase your confidence in what you are good at, why you're good at it, and most importantly what responsibilities to ask your leaders for.

O—Optimizing Leaders

Managers manage people and tasks; giving orders without developing connection or legacy. Leaders produce other leaders… optimizing their leadership and the leadership skills within members of their organization, team, family, and relationships.

Look at any successful sports team. The successful head coach is always in the news and interviews, but quietly many of the coaches under them soon leave the organization, get their own head coaching jobs, become successful, and a Coaching Tree is formed! Why? Because leaders produce other leaders! They bring in people who are hungry, ready to learn, are aware of their own superpower, get more and more rope, and off they go to success! This only happens when the leader is willing to let go of the rope a bit to see what happens, see what's great, and what needs to be fine-tuned.

If you are looking for more rope, a request may sound like "Hi
_____, I want to be great here. I believe my superpower/best asset
is _____ and I want to be of more value and impact. I'd like
to start _____ and would like a week (you pick the
timeframe) to do my best and then get your feedback. Does that sound
reasonable?". No matter the response, you will learn a lot from their
answer. You'll either get more rope or exit the conversation with a new
understanding of what they'd like you to know more of or an idea if this
company, team, or relationship is for you.

P—Prioritize Your Time by Letting Go

"Busy" doesn't mean "Better" and "Busy" most certainly doesn't
always mean productive. Too many times we get caught being "Busy"
instead of "Better" and keeping the rope and all of the stress that comes
will it all to ourselves. So, what to do?

The answer is to prioritize your time. I often share the concept of
my Priority Quadrant when working with companies and employees,
in my past blogs, and also in my videos on social media. I won't go into
depth, but it simply breaks down to your priorities fitting into:

1. High Priority/Handle Now
2. High Priority/Handle Later
3. Lower Priority/Handle Now
4. Lower Priority/Handle Later

If you're in a position of leadership, sometimes it can feel as though
everything is in the High Priority/Handle Now Quadrant but it's not.
In looking at your list of responsibilities, perhaps it makes sense to let go
and give a bit of rope within your Lower Priority/Handle Later or Lower
Priority/Handle Now. As you gain more trust and traction, perhaps the
High Priority/Handle Later; freeing up more time for you to develop
leaders and more time for your people to become leaders. Imagine
a parent doing every task for their kids; then complaining that their

children don't know how to do anything, are ungrateful, and unaware of what it takes to get anything and EVERYTHING done. What?!?

E—Easy on the Consequences

As you give more rope; there will be growing pains, incidents of mistakes, misunderstandings, and plain ol' big blunders! Remember, it's par for the course! Going heavy on the consequences, insults, rolling of the eyes, or any of the other demeaning acts that act to snatch the rope back only hinders growth. The key here is to understand why the mistakes happen, their mode of thinking, showing the bigger picture, and teaching ways to best move forward!

I don't promise the Leader's R. O. P. E. to be easy, but I do promise it to be worth it as you work to develop leaders, place them in the right-seats using their superpowers, enhancing their powers with your own, and evolving both leadership and work/life harmony for you and them!

"Managers manage people and tasks; giving orders without developing connection or legacy. Leaders produce other leaders... optimizing their leadership and the leadership skills within members of their organization, team, family, and relationships."

– Andre Young

CHAPTER 32
A Leader's Algebra

I cannot begin to tell you how much I despised the subject of Math during my school-age years. Then came Algebra and that despise escalated to hate. I know... hate is a very strong word and I rarely use it, but in this case, it was true! Algebra and I were... and still are bitter foes. I wouldn't say I couldn't do Algebra, because a true "Can't" is rare. The truth is more I didn't want to, I didn't like it, and I didn't care about it. However, as I've evolved, I have come to value the power and impact of formulas and effective processes. If you are looking to enhance your leadership, professionally and personally, there are two simple equations that will allow us to enhance our personal leadership, our surrounding culture, lifestyle, and overall joy. So, what are they?

Equation 1: Don't Add Positive to Negative

Professionally: Every organization wants to add the "Inspired & Motivated" employee to their team; the individual that is eager to learn, make an impact, work their tail off, display leadership qualities, hungry to advance and make an impact. Yes, these individuals are awesome, you wish everyone you hire could be this way, and I encourage you to hire as many of these people as you can, but before you do… they're two things to consider.

Is your company's culture capable of satisfying and keeping these Allstars? Be mindful that you're not adding positive people to a negative culture. If the negative culture is bigger than what the positive person/people can handle you will either not have the positive people for long or they will begin to drain, burn-out, bore-out, and become a part of the Negative Nick and Nancy Club! That is truly the saddest thing to see in a company… when a former "Inspired & Motivated" employee becomes a problematic cog due to ignoring this simple equation. In short, attention to Culture-Care is as important as the "Inspired and Motivated" you are seeking!

It's important for those in positions of leadership to know that the "Inspired & Motivated" are looking for great leaders and leadership they can respect, count on, and evolve in. Therefore, the Allstar you want to hire will be expecting more out of you… pushing you to be the leader you sold yourself to be throughout the interview process.

Before founding my company, *You Evolving Now* and becoming a speaker and author, I was a Mental Health Therapist. The clients that came in knowing what they wanted to get out of therapy, who were already in action-phase, and eager to make progress were the clients that made sure you were on you're A-Game. I took pride in always providing the best service and impact possible, but these individuals expected more, were ready, wanted results, and effective strategies in session and for homework. In short, if you are bringing in great people; pay them back with great leadership… being curious enough to know what they would like out of the experience, being willing to speak their language, and helping them to be of impact!

Personally: We all have life going on and it can be quite the rollercoaster! If your life is in chaos and dysfunction… be mindful of adding positive people to your dysfunction if you are not dedicated to your own evolution; depending on them or the relationship to give you a break from your dysfunction, or expecting them to take your dysfunction away. It's not fair, not their job, and without your effort in your life... it will chisel away your respect for them and burn them out in the process.

Seeking and welcoming positive and "good-vibed" people into your life is a good thing, but only healthy if you're willing to do your own work, learn with them, and enhance your personal leadership, leadership skills, and work/life harmony.

Equation 2: Subtract then Add

Subtraction often gets a negative wrap. Most people don't want less; the less home, the less car, less income, etc. While in contrast, more home, more income, more employees, more projects, more, more, more sounds better... but is it?

Professionally: There is power is subtracting. Before you add new hires and all of the new "Inspired & Motivated" perhaps it's wise to subtract the dysfunctional employees first. Subtract the processes that aren't producing much or not working at all... and see what happens when you are left with the people that actually want to be there, want to work, have been looking for opportunity within the organization, and are welcoming change. The 80/20 rule states that 20% of your people do 80% of the work... so are MORE subpar or negative people really necessary? Let's see how things are with a more efficient and trimmed staff... then hire the "Inspired & Motivated"; welcoming them into a well-run, promising, positive-culture machine!

Personally: For most people, it feels good to have that special relationship, that significant other you can count on... even if the relationship is unhealthy, or that group of friends you've outgrown or are bored with. It's always amazed me what we can allow ourselves to get comfortable with! However, if you're interested in having the life and lifestyle of your dreams... it starts with enhancing your personal leadership… and that can be hard to do within the relationship you are already in. I'm not suggesting you cut anyone… that's a rare thing we need to do! I am suggesting you get comfortable getting great on your own without depending on a buddy or a relationship. Subtract some time out of your day and life to get great! You want to lose weight, get comfortable doing it by yourself. You want to learn something new, get comfortable reading alone at night when everyone goes to bed… you get the point!

If you are in transition, between relationships or friendships… good! It's a perfect time to "Subtract then Add"! Be mindful of your new-found alone time… what will you intentionally schedule into your day allowing you to learn, grow, and evolve; preparing you to walk into your new friendships and relationship better instead of bitter, better instead of blaming, and ready to impact instead of waiting to be saved!

Alone time can be an exciting time… depending on what you choose to do with it! Enjoy becoming the leader you are capable of professionally and personally; your Future-Self will thank you for it!

"It's important for those in positions of leadership to know that the "Inspired & Motivated" are looking for great leaders and leadership they can respect, count on, and evolve in."

– Andre Young

CHAPTER 33

A Leader's Priorities:
The Priorities Quadrant

I pride myself on being a hard-worker, a smart-worker, dedicated to my craft, and on top of my priorities... both professionally and personally. That's why, this topic... A Leader's Priority, is one of my biggest pet peeves! The only way to evolve through a pet peeve or on-going frustrating event is to understand it better and plan with anticipation to positively manage it when it inevitably rears its head.

In any job, there will be a list of duties and expectations that come with it. The manner in which the duties and expectations are fulfilled or unfulfilled will determine your reputation. Each task has its own level of priority; some are of the utmost priority and need to be handled right away, of the utmost priority but must wait; while some are of lower priority but would benefit from being handled right away, ending with tasks of lower priority and can be handled later. All are priorities, but not all need your attention right now... nor can all of your attention be adequately given to each! Before we move on to my pet peeve and what to do... let's take a look at The Leader's Priority Quadrant. Where do your priorities fit and how will you move forward allowing an evolution in your leadership and work/life harmony?

1. *High Priority / Handle Now*—This is a task or issue of monumental functional and/or financial significance impacting your company or relationship and needs to be addressed right now to either reap great reward or suffer great loss!

2. *High Priority /Handle Later*—This is an issue of monumental significance, but there is not much you can do about it right away. Perhaps a meeting is set in the near or distant future or your work is done and you're awaiting the work of someone else in order to move forward in the process.

3. *Lower Priority / Handle Now*—Lower priority does not mean not important or significant; rather, your action may not produce immediate desired benefits or production, but if you put it off... it may never get done and any potential impact is missed... Example: The handwritten Thank You cards sent out to the person/family/company you sold to in order to maintain a personal touch and on-going relationship.

4. *Lower Priority /Handle Later*—Again, lower priority doesn't mean it's not important and shouldn't be addressed or completed. This category suggests you have a long list of things to do. What doesn't fit into the other categories... ends up here. The important thing to note is... you must come up with a reasonable time frame for when "Later" is. This is the list that will pile up and hurt you the most in the end. Neglected, this is a trash pile of all the hidden and minute details that help to drive a company or relationship into the ground. Fulfilled, these are the dotted I's and crossed T's that propel you into greatness.

   Note: This is the Quadrant you may want to consider delegating to others to help enhance your leadership skills and theirs!

My pet peeve is struck when leaders act as if everything that needs to be done is lumped into the High Priority/Handle Now Category! I've been on both sides of the fence... as an employee and as a business owner. It's a sad day when an "Inspired and Motivated" employee burnsout because their "To-Do List" became unbearable, unrealistic, and unmanageable. The paradox is, everything is important and a priority, but everything cannot be a now priority... and great leaders know that!

As an employee, I remember being promoted to a position of leadership. I chose to hold onto some of my pre-existing responsibilities and accepted the additional duties of my new position. As the organization grew and changed; so did my responsibilities... and so did my life. I used to take work home to stay on pace; completing work at night or weekends. However, as my children grew... my free time shrank! I began compressing all of the work into a workday with a boss that believed everything was of high priority and needed to be handled now.

I was later asked why something (I can't remember what it was) wasn't done. It was the last straw for me. My response was, "Are you really asking why it isn't done or are you telling me to get it done?". I also asked, "What is/are the top one, two, or three priorities of my role?' seeking clarification on what was the most important thing/s that needs to be done and completed. It's very easy to become busy, but if our quadrants don't match with our boss, employees, and mission... we will only be busy being frustrated and feeling under-appreciated. Although this led to a great open and honest conversation, I'm not suggesting you say what I said. What I am suggesting is leaders, employers, employees, and those in relationships understand that EVERYTHING cannot be of High Priority/Handle Now. So what to do?

Prioritize

As a leader, are you putting everything that needs to get done in the High Priority/ Handle Now Category for yourself and your people to deal with? In your business, work-life, and in your personal life where does everything fit, what needs to be addressed right away and every day, weekly, and checked-in on. Are your expectations of your people reasonable, doable, and fair? Remember… just because you'd do it, sacrificing all your time, relationships, and lifestyle for your passion… doesn't me they need to, should have to, or that it's their passion and dream.

Solution

Although I was under tremendous pressure and dissatisfaction in the example I used when I was an employee, I was wrong in two major areas. I chose to bring along responsibilities from my old position. Some of us have a hard time letting go. I enjoyed the hands-on task of my former position. It's what I was great at and born to do, but the promotion was where the money was and positions of so-called glory. Note: So many are promoted into positions of leadership, not because they know how to lead, but because they do one thing great; later to cause a communication and culture problem within organizations. As an employee, I owed it to my company to put my ego aside and allow them to be aware the additional duties were negatively impacting me. I also could have done a better job of putting my staff in the right-seats to match their superpowers. Being open, honest, and delegating appropriately is the key to protecting yourself and your people from Burn-Out!

Secondly, I could have beat my company to the punch by offering a suggested solution to the problem. Emerging leaders listen up… instead of complaining, gossiping and earning your Negative Nick or Nancy Badge… constructively address only the people that can help and make a difference. Also, accompany your problem with a suggested solution. When I became a business owner, this became one of my "3 Rules". I trusted my staff to know their craft and their audience and was willing to listen to problems… but only if they were accompanied with suggested solutions. Either my socks would be blown-off due to their feedback and we'd go with their solution, we'd compromise on an idea, or I'd explain why we couldn't move forward due to bigger-picture issues they may have not been aware of. Either way... I was open to being aware, they were heard, and we improved!

Follow-Up

If you or someone is living in High Priority/ Handle Now Mode they tend to be high stress and anxious most of the time. If this individual chooses to either put their ego aside to speak to you positively and maturely or if they blew up on you due to stress and you've resolved it... please follow-up! This is a step that can easily fall into the Lower Priority/Handle Later Quadrant because you may not think it's a big deal and you can push it off until their annual review, but it will mean a lot to them. Perhaps it's a Lower Priority/Handle Now as you decide to ask how everything is, how they are handling the workload, if there's anything they need from you, and speak their Leader's 7 Langauge (explained later in this book). This is bonding, evolving, and leadership!

Whether you're in a position of leadership within an organization, team, or leading your own life and relationship... you have your priorities, other people have there's... do they match? Are your people aware of yours? Are you of theirs? The saddest and one of the most common reasons for the demise of professional or personal relationships is when both parties are motivated, willing, and moving full-speed ahead doing things they think are important to the other person... and it's not.

"The paradox is, everything is a priority but everything cannot be a now priority... great leaders know that."
– Andre Young

CHAPTER 34

A Leader's Apology

Apologizing... for some is the hardest thing in the world! For others... it's the easiest and every other word is "I'm sorry". The question is... "Why"? Apologizing tends to deals with our pride, self-image, and status. As a leader, if these three things are not intact and healthy... apologizing can make you feel weak, lesser than, vulnerable, and victim to the persecution and power of the person you are apologizing to. However, an apology done correctly and for the right reason does the opposite... leaving you feeling powerful, accountable, lighter, and more comfortable with leaving the ball in the other person's court.

First and most importantly... We cannot be above apologizing! Can you remember a time when a person of authority apologized to you and didn't have to due to their position? How did it feel? Perhaps it was your parents, your coach, your boss, a police officer... whomever it was... it was powerful as they chose to admit wrong-doing, misjudgment, and voluntarily made themselves equals as a human being outside of their authority. Let's be able and willing to give that gift to the people we lead!

To understand the art of giving and receiving an apology we must start here... there is a difference between being truly sorry and simply wanting things to go back to the way they were. Although the status quo may be comfortable, no one or any relationship can stay the same. Through our life experiences and the roller-coaster of life... things change. Be careful not to invest your time and energy in trying to recreate an over-romanticized past. Invest in the future to move forward and EVOLVE! A "Sorry" without intent to be different or better is futile leadership.

A true apology implies understanding, incorporates strength, and a plan. While an unprocessed sorry can imply feelings of remorse; without understanding why the situation occurred and how the other person was impacted; leading to the likelihood of situation repeating itself: Why did this happen? Why would I or someone do that or say what was said or done? What were they thinking, feeling, and experiencing at that time to make that decision? Be Mindful... An unprocessed "Sorry" is equivalent to placing a band-aid on a bullet wound.

A Leader's Apology is work on YOUR part... Beginning with the understanding of YOUR "Why". When the event occurred... you had thoughts that ran through your mind... some too quick to catch and others that got stuck, leading you to perseverate and act. These thoughts made you angry, hurt, scared, fearful, etc. THEN... you lashed out and hurt someone. An evolved apology does not simply cover what you said and did... it also explains what you were thinking and how you were feeling.

Second—Understand your patterns. When you're hurt, scared, offended, intimidated, or anxious as a leader... you have a pattern and tend to act and react in the same way most of the time. To be "Sorry" you must understand your pattern, take responsibility for your pattern, and work to evolve your pattern… not simply cradle your self-righteous pain of being "Busy" and ignore the valid points presented by others.

Third—Understand the other persons "WHY" and their pattern. Notice… I did not say agree with their "WHY" or the behavior. The point here is to listen, understand, and honor that they are a person with their own history, baggage, thoughts, feelings, and patterns. WE are not the only person in the equation!

Fourth—Apologize! Apologies don't have "Buts", However, they have they do have boundaries! For example, "I'm sorry I talked behind your back and damaged your reputation, but you…". I don't have to finish this sentence, because anything after "But" is bull and no one hears anything after you blamed them, made it their fault, and you didn't accept accountability.

An apology is "I'm sorry I talked bad about you. I was having a terrible day and was frustrated by how things have been. I vented to everyone and that wasn't right; as I know people look at me as an example. It won't happen again and I'm sorry". I know… it sounds cheesy, but this is very close to an apology I once gave in the workplace before I was Mr. You Evolving Now and the leader I am today! Feel free to use this and make it your own; as it covers all of the necessary parts of a Leader's Apology!

Fifth—Boundaries… not ultimatums! A boundary states self-respect, relationship- respect, and a willingness to enhance mutual understanding. Ultimatums make you the boss, one person having the power, and egg-shells have been dropped all over the floor of your relationship… making it increasingly tense and uncomfortable for the other person to exist, be themselves, and enjoy. A boundary says… for US to continue the relationship, It's important for me to_____ because _____. How do you feel about that? If yes… great! If not they're sure… is there room for compromise? If No… you and that person have a decision to either continue as is or part ways.

An apology is NOT a minimization, justification, or rationalization of your behavior. It's a gift to the offended and the wronged… and a gift for you as a leader; allowing a sense of humbleness, accountability, a lighter feeling, and hopefully an opportunity to create a new normal!

"Apologies don't have "Buts"… However, they do have boundaries."

– Andre Young

WAY TO LEAD 5

A LEADER'S RISK

CHAPTER 35

A Leader's Risky Evolution

As a child, everything is a risk... from taking our first steps, learning to ride a bike, going to school on the first day, transitioning to new schools, our first love, picking a college, deciding our future path, getting married, and more! It takes a lot of risk, courage, and bumps and bruises to the body and soul to have gotten where you are today. However, as adults, somewhere along the way you may have stopped taking as many risks. And there can be a number of reasons! Maybe you're comfortable where you are and no risks are needed. Perhaps you're fearful of taking the risk and failing. Maybe you've taken risks before and been burned. Whatever your reason... I will admit, not every risk needs to be taken... but a life without risk can easily lead to boredom, stagnation, droning, and regret.

As a leader, you have a dream, a goal, and a desired lifestyle... whatever your dream... IT WILL REQUIRE SOME RISK! Risking your comfort, your heart, your money, your identity, and most likely your time, energy, and effort. When you're ready to risk… it's beneficial to understand… Risk does not always equal success. It does not promise your dream life at work, at home, or in your relationships. Risk only promises you different short-term experiences. How you process, learn from, and apply those series of different short-term experiences will lead to your success. As you EVOLVE through the process of risk-taking… you may be surprised how your definition of success may alter. The picture you have of success is nice… and proves to be a great starting point, but if that exact picture is the only thing that will make you happy and satisfied YOU are setting YOURSELF up for disaster.

Remember, every risk isn't for everyone. It is up to you to evaluate the risk for you, your team, and the people it will impact. When you decide to go for it… prepare yourself and your team to push a bit past the comfort zone and enjoy the positives of EVOLUTION; allowing time to celebrate successes and accept each set-back as a "Success Lesson"!

"Risk doesn't promise success. It only promises you different short-term experiences. How you choose to process, learn from, and apply those series of different short-term experiences will lead you to success."

– Andre Young

CHAPTER 36
How to Take a R. I. S. K.

R isk... one of the 4-letter words in our society! So many of us are scared of taking risks; not because we don't want to reach our definition of success but because of fear and anxiety related to change and potential loss. As a leader, after evaluating the risk of adding, subtracting, and moving forward... we must choose to live through and beyond our fear and anxiety of change! Fear will stall you, your life, your relationships, your success, your dream, and your leadership... keeping you safe, but also keeping you small.

It's easy to take failure or slow success personally, as we tend to think "See, I tried and I failed; I'm a____(whatever horrible thing you're going to say, think, and believe about yourself)_____". The truth is... failure is all about how you choose to perceive it! View failure as an opportunity to find out what works and what doesn't work for you and your team... and why! Failure is a necessary building tool to our true path to a destination you never could have imagined for your work, your team, your family, and your life! To accept the risk is also to accept CHANGE. Leaders accept feeling uncomfortable for a while… It's called "Growing Pains" for a reason!

It has always amazed me what we can allow ourselves to get comfortable with! That safe success in your business that barely pays the bills, but as long as the lights are on… no need for risk. That idea you have that people are paying for right now… but what about 3 years from now? That relationship you drone home to, talking poorly about all day long, and don't even make eye-contact in. The list goes on… The important thing to note is… if you're thinking of taking a positive risk in your life… you are NOT happy where you are anyway… so change your view on failure, keep reading, and let's jump!

The most important concept for you to know about risk is… most risks do not equal immediate success! Unless you are that lucky person that bought the winning lottery ticket and your new life as a multi-millionaire begins tomorrow! Rather, as I mentioned in the previous chapter, risk equals a new short-term experience. When you take a risk and begin to live your new lifestyle… you will encounter new thoughts, feelings, people, events, and experiences. How YOU process them, take advantage of them, learn, apply, and EVOLVE over time will create your new success!

Here's a breakdown of R. I. S. K.; allowing you to EVOLVE as a leader:

R—Ready

Most people will make necessary changes in their life when they absolutely have to! When the pain or annoyance gets too high to endure, they are at their rock-bottom, or when their line in the sand is crossed for the millionth time. Everyone you care about can tell you to make changes and take risks, but YOU will do it when you're ready and in your time. However, when you can force yourself to be a bit more proactive instead of reactive… you can get to where you are going a lot faster and in a lot less pain! Help yourself EVOLVE and get ready by making a plan, literally putting it in your phone calendar with alerts, and tell people of the changes you will make; keeping you accountable to your personal leadership and mission!

I—Intelligent

You want to take a risk, enhance your personal leadership skills, and overall leadership to EVOLVE? Become an intentional learner about the thing you want to do. Knowledge breeds confidence! What are the various ways and the best way for you to expand your vision? Whatever your risk is… get intentional about upping your intellect in that area!

My sons are both basketball players and want to play at a high level in college and beyond. However, when I walk past their room… they are on their game system, scrolling through YouTube or on their game system. Be aware that being entertained all the time is counterproductive to your dream and your leadership. Instead of vilifying social media and technology… let's use it! I suggested my boys YouTube or Google how to shoot a great jump shot, basketball tutorials, coaches' comments, etc. It's all there on the same device they already have in their hand! Needless to say, the addition of new information and a willingness to apply it has made big impact for my boys and their ball game! Take your phone out, search up your dream, learn more, do it daily, and BOOM!

S—Skills

Skills pay the bills! You will need the skills to do whatever you are desiring to do. Ambition without ability can only take you so far… otherwise, everyone would be in the NFL, a Michael Jordan, a Steve Jobs, an Oprah Winfrey, a famous rapper, etc. The good thing about skills are… you can improve your skills, but not always your ambition. Learn, Apply, Build, to EVOLVE! What skills do you want to improve? What skills would you like the individuals on your team to improve? Do they know that… or does that only come up in the dreaded Annual Review? I often coach players and employees on how to make their leaders lead them better or to help their coaches coach them better. As a true leader, let's be mindful to be ahead of the game… consistently upping our skills and our team! Later in this book, you're going to learn the greatest Preface Statement of all time; along with the Leader's 7 to make conversations like these much easier!

K—Keen

You must have a keen sense of when to stay on your path and when to alter to a new path. As you begin to take risks and EVOLVE in your new short-term experiences you will be faced with new options. This will be in the form of new people, new ideas, new ventures… some good, some bad, some dead-ends, and some that may be short-term wins or long-term wins. Stay in tune with yourself, your personal mission, the bigger picture, and your desired lifestyle; making decisions based on that. Enjoy the process!

> *"Leaders are in-tuned with themselves, their personal mission, the bigger picture, and their desired lifestyle; making decisions based on that."*
>
> **– Andre Young**

CHAPTER 37

Managing C. H. A. N. G. E.

C hange can be a scary word... can't it? It implies us doing something different than what we've normally done and have become accustomed to. Even if the change is positive, it carries feelings of anxiety, pressure, and possibly resentment... especially depending on why change is being made! As I said, it always amazes me how comfortable we can become with anything! Comfortable with eating unhealthy even though we know what it's doing to our body and the eventual results. Comfortable in that "bad" relationship and hanging in there to the bitter end. Or, so comfortable in our success, we stop growing and give up greatness for "good enough". At any rate... change, whether for the positive or negative... is expensive and will cost us either our EFFORT as payment for the great... or a lifetime payment of REGRET for our stagnation. If you're ready for more... ready to evolve your leadership... and want to know how to manage the change you think you want and the change you don't want ... keep reading for how to C. H. A. N. G. E.!

To positively change, overcome the initial discomfort, and maintain your effort you must start with the 3 C's of Change:

C—Constant

The first… and most important thing we must respect and understand about change is that it's constant… It has to happen! Change is one of the few things that is inevitable, but yet seems to shock us every time it happens. Once we can accept that change is a part of life and will rarely occur the way we want it; or in our time frame the better off we will be.

Your sweet baby will grow to be that teenager with their own thoughts and way of looking at the world. That job you loved may eventually breed new management, policies, and expectations you never expected. That partner you married will eventually become a mother or father and you're going to see them in a whole new light… for better and for worse… It's CHANGE and it's forever constant. As you've been reading this book… I hope you remember the purpose is to enhance your Work/Life Harmony and become a better Leader. This is a major factor of growth… being able to anticipate the obvious change and prepare as much as possible; as not to be upset, dejected, and miserable when it occurs because you knew it was coming!

When I present this topic on stage, I often share a pretend story of you waking out of your home in the morning and halfway down the street… a stranger jumps out and punches you in the face. Now that's a shock! Who could have anticipated that? The next day, you wake-up, leave the house, walk down the same street and … BAM! You get hit in the face again. What the heck? The next day… I would hope you'd do something different. Perhaps walk down a different street, hit the person back, or learn to bob and weave! Keep your eyes wide open in your 4 P's as a Person, a Professional, a Partner, and Parent… what keeps punching you in the face? What can you anticipate happening over the next year or so?

Many people saw the writing on the wall at their job or in that relationship that things were going to change and did nothing expect choose to ride it out, become a victim, and succumb to misery. Leaders see change, anticipate change, prepare as much as possible for change, and dominate change… refusing to let change dominate them!

C—Consistent

In the face of the change you want: getting that job, that promotion, that raise, that starting position on the sports team, that new relationship… and in the face of the change you didn't want: not getting the promotion or raise, the starting spot, ending the relationship… our choice to be consistent is the same! What do I mean by consistent? Choosing to show up with a smile, do your best, and being your best! I've mentioned this several times because it's that important!

Success can change us; either swelling our ego or stressing us out with the unexpected amount of new responsibilities that come with success. At a job, rarely will people pay you more for doing less… so you got that promotion… with 200+ more emails per day to respond to. You earned the starting position and now are in a leadership role on and off the field; and are the model for hard-work and dedication. You get the point! Or, you didn't get the promotion, raise, or starting spot, and the moments of not getting our way may not always build character… but it will always reveal it.

My youngest son plays quarterback. When he made up his mind to play the position, I explained only one quarterback gets to play at a time. You're either the starting quarterback or you're on the sideline holding a clipboard. It's unlike any other position in sports. He assured me he was a quarterback… So, I said OK! At some point, he may have to face the disappointment of someone outplaying him, or a coach that prefers another player, or a system that isn't tailored to or for him… it's what I call "A Leader's Anticipation"; anticipating that it's (or something like it has to eventually happen) going to happen at some point… it has to… and CHOOSING to consistently show up daily with a smile and positive attitude, doing his best and learning his craft, and being his best as a great person on and off the field!

Yes, this is much easier said than done, but what's the alternative? Becoming a cynical grouch, a destructive cog in the system, and being ill-prepared to succeed and exceed expectations when called upon. I guess that is an option... one that many people take, but not you, not the leader that you have become! Perhaps one day... you will leave that job, leave that relationship, or switch teams... you wouldn't be the first and certainly won't be the last to do so... but do it with grace and intentional preparation be great elsewhere!

C—Confidence

You must develop a vision of your desired lifestyle as well as a confidence through self-love that you CAN and WILL move forward! You may be ready and willing to sprint toward that vision... or you may only be able to crawl, but forward is forward! If you are not ready to love yourself, have confidence in yourself, or you're simply tired of grinding... that's OK. Rest for a while, lean on someone that loves you, is willing to support you, but most importantly motivate, inspire, and kick you in the butt to reach your protentional! This would imply you being ready and willing to build a team around you with positive, motivated, and more successful people than you. It's very difficult to change with negative "stuck" people around you all the time!

H—Humility

This is monumentally important. Most people who want to change are embarrassed about where they currently are: maybe their job, the money they make, the way they look, their past, etc. Humility means you are willing and capable of acknowledging and owning EXACTLY where you are, accepting it for now, deciding what you will do about it, and doing something about it daily! Get over yourself... you may not be where you'd like to be, but there are a million people who'd be more than happy to trade places with you RIGHT NOW!

Humility also refers to maintaining empathy. As you're going through change… so are your co-workers, your employees or staff, your partner, and your kids? Can you remember what it was like to be new to the job, the person who wanted the promotion… but someone else got it instead, remember being a teenager and all of the drama that was soooo important or how life wasn't really important at all because you were incapable of seeing or respecting the "Big Picture"? Well, that's where they are now! What would you have wanted or needed to hear from someone in your position to enlighten and support you?

A—Action

This is as simple as I can make it. You are what you THINK… leading to what you FEEL, leading to what you DO! You are your patterns… so what does your daily pattern say about you? Get active and DO something about your passion and goal daily!

Action and Change are also split into two areas… and here are two different formulas for each!

The Change You Can Control

As a Leader in your 4 P's, if you are in control of upcoming change, try this formula to make the impact you desire; while also including and empowering other leaders:

Brainstorm—Come up with ideas that will make a positive impact!

Decide—Choose the best idea/s that are most impactful!

Collaborate—Get feedback from the people it will be affecting!

Implement—Start the idea!

Collaborate—Check-In with the people that are using and doing the idea!

Fine-Tune—Make any necessary adjustments to enhance and EVOLVE!

Repeat—Start the process all over again!

The Change You Cannot Control

Sometimes, even as a Leader... There are some things out of our control. Sometimes, change and life circumstances will dictate what needs to happen next. For example... At work, by time the news of change gets to you... the train may have already left the station... All Aboard! When change is out of our control... Try this:

Inform—Let others know what's happening, why, the benefit, and EMPATHY!

Educate—Be transparent with the positives, the negatives, and the new direction!

Plan—Share the plan for success and everyone's' part in the plan to make it work!

Train—Be sure everyone knows HOW TO DO IT!

EVOLVE Together—Maintain the WE by being present and available for all!

N—Nursing

Through Change, we will all encounter obstacles both big and small. Some we will breeze through, some we will trip over that bruise our spirit and ego, but we will learn from it all! Be sure to take time to nurse your wounds... there is value in rest and healing. Be sure while you're resting and healing, you're taking mental notes on why you fell, what you learned, and what you'll do next time! Be sure... you WILL see that obstacle again, but next time you'll be prepared!

G—Growth

Change is inevitable, but growth isn't! I repeat, Growth is not a given! Change will happen, but we must choose to grow! If everyone who started the process of change would automatically grow, there would be no unhappy, unsatisfied, or bitter people in the world. Everyone has attempted change whether in the slightest form or biggest form.

Your growth will depend on your willingness to "Keep your eyes wide-open" as you go through new experiences. "Keeping your eyes-wide-open" means you take in every experience... both good and bad to learn, grow, and improve. If you fail at something, after licking your wounds... you realize you have just gone through an experience that will allow you to help someone else and yourself in the future! What did you learn from the failure and how will you impart that knowledge into your future success? The same goes for your success! If you don't know why you succeeded, how can you do it again and mentor those who are following you?

E—Excitement

This is your life... the only one you get to live! You might as well be excited about it! To effectively change... you must know yourself and set realistic little goals to get to your dream. If you want to get in good cardio shape, but hate the gym and love shopping... Then don't go to the gym! Go to the mall and count your steps. Or go to the gym and reward yourself with a trip to the mall! Get creative with yourself and stay excited about your "Why" and create a process that pushes you, and brings you feelings of increased self-worth!

What excites you? Perhaps it is your job, your dream, learning something new about your craft or hobby, seeing your significant other after a long day, seeing your kids, or treating yourself to something cool because you chose to beat the day instead of letting it beat you! Whatever you choose... wake up tomorrow excited about the life you get to live!

"As a leader, after evaluating the risk of adding and subtracting to move forward... we must choose to live through and beyond our fear and anxiety of change."
– Andre Young

CHAPTER 38

How to Lead when H. U. R. T.

Leadership, whether we are talking about being in a position of leadership in your professional life or choosing to be a leader of your own life personally… I think we can agree that it's easier to lead when we feel our best, when everything is going our way, and our wants and needs are being met! It's easy to lead in times like these, but life cannot and will not stay that way for long! You are going to go through hurt and trying times and WHEN you do, will you still lead and be a leader that you and your people can respect? Perhaps your pain is coming from being unrecognized and underappreciated at work, disliking your job, being "Burnt-Out" or "Bored-Out" professionally or personally, maybe you're going through a breakup or divorce, a loss in your family, financial stress and worrying how you're going to eat, or a serious health concern. In these times, can you… will you… still lead? I've had the pain and privilege of living, leading, and evolving through each of these scenarios and also assisting others through the process. Here's how to Lead when H. U. R. T.!

H—Heal

Choosing to heal is the first step! Notice I said choosing... The name of my company is You Evolving Now; not You Evolving Later. Healing is a verb; of course, time is a factor but your intentional and consistent effort to this first process will act to collapse time frames; allowing you to learn more about you and evolve while you're feeling your feelings. Remember... Feelings are strong, but they are secondary to our thoughts! What you think will impact how you feel, then what you do, then the consequences thereafter... either negative or positive!

In the process of choosing to heal, here a few concepts that will impact your life:

Self-Healing

Healing is your job, not the job of others! If we need the official apology from our employee, employer, partner, or kids to happen... or to happen the way we believe we deserve in order to heal and move on... you will never heal! Choose to heal because it's best for you, your life, your relationships, your dreams, and your desired lifestyle! What would be the point of achieving your definition of success and still being bitter, empty, and alone?

Why?

This is a hard point... WHY did the hurt occur? Sometimes, life just stinks and horrible things happened to good people. Other times, we can see how our actions or inaction was partly to blame for our pain. Perhaps you've neglected certain professional or personal responsibilities, behaved in unbecoming manners, only gave the minimal; ignoring the needs of others that would have propelled you along. Whatever the reason... True Leaders accept full responsibility for their part, Acknowledging, Accepting, and Deciding what they will do next... learning from their hurt and evolving toward their dream and desired lifestyle!

Forgiveness

Yes, Forgiveness... but please realize, forgiveness is a choice! If you choose not to forgive... it's OK, but you are also choosing to continue to feel the way you do about your boss, your employee/s, partner, kids, or whomever. If you do choose, it's not as simple as just letting things go. I find many people struggle with forgiveness because they think that's what it is. Forgiveness is a process:

1. Share Your Story—Whatever happened professionally or personally is hurtful to you and made an impact. However, most people will go around and tell their story and pain to everyone and anyone at work and in their personal lives who will listen! That only perpetuates pain; making you feel more righteously justified to do less and be less. Be mindful to share your story with a selected people that will not only listen, but also challenge, and be an agent of you moving forward! It's human nature to vent... you vent, I vent, we all vent... but leaders practice what I call "Controlled Venting"; making your venting people-limited, time-limited, and evolved-focused!

2. Understanding Your Offenders "Why"—There are very few monsters in the world... they do exist, but there are few! Most people aren't waking up with you on their mind with evil plans to ruin your day and your day only. Assuming most people are good and most people have enough of their own stuff (professionally and personally) going on... the question becomes, "Why would that person say, do, or act the way they did?", "What could be going on in their world or their HURT that would make this happen?". Of course, this does not excuse behavior; rather provides deeper understanding, empathy, patience, and a bit of a pause for your reaction!

3. Boundary Setting—Forgiveness is not a sign of weakness; it's a sign of strength... not only to forgive but to also uphold new boundaries that work to protect you, your leadership, and your dreams! You may choose to forgive your boss, employee, co-worker, partner, etc.... but not without a new boundary. Is there a boundary that is reasonable, doable, and fair that you need to continue the relationship? If yes and they are adaptable... great! If not, it may be time to part ways with peace of mind and your leadership and reputation intact!

4. Let it Go—Now it's time to allow TIME to do its thing. After a healthy process of professional or personal forgiveness... let time make "Letting it Go" easier. However, be mindful of how often or how negatively you choose to share your past hurt with others. It's hard for a scar to heal if you keep picking at it. Gross, but you get the point!

Dream Living!

To heal... only to live a mundane life; doing only the "Have-To's" of your day... going to a job instead of your passion, carting kids around, cooking the same meals, doing laundry... only to wake up and do it until you die is not living!

Be sure your Dream is in your Daily! What is your dream, your definition of success, and your expanded definition of success? Too many times, I ask people what their dream is and they give me one answer they believe will make them happy and fulfilled. Life is bigger than that. What is your dream and definition of success as a person, a partner, parent, professional, son/daughter, sibling, friend, etc.? Whatever you need to do to do your part in achieving that definition... schedule it into your day!

Of course, it would be stressful to address all of your dreams in one day... so be faithful to your dream in its general state. In the past my specific dream was to have my own business, it had to look a certain way, I had to make a certain amount of money, and the path had to look how I saw it in my head. As I evolved, I realized the "generalness" of my dream was more important, healthy, reasonable, and doable. My dream is to support my family with ideas and concepts I've created within and for the structure of my own business. Therefore, I create daily (writing or making videos), I read to hone my craft daily, I make numerous business contacts daily, and I'm sure to be consistent (the same off stage as when you meet me at the grocery store)! My dream is to also have an awesome marriage and show my kids a great and healthy relationship. Therefore, I'm sure to intentionally love to my wife daily.

Are you living or doing something about your dream daily? Is it scheduled in the calendar or on your phone with alerts and notifications? Perhaps your dream is a promotion, to start your own business, have a great relationship, get a house... Whatever it is; what do you have to learn, how can you raise your personal or professional value, and what will you do about it daily? Lastly, it's hard to live your dream daily with poor, non-helpful, dream-killing language. Speak positively about your starting point, where you and your team are, where you're going, and be eager to win each day! You'd be surprised how your hurt starts to subside, who you begin to attract, and the inspiration you become for others.

U—Understanding the Opposition

I developed my R.E.U. Way years ago and use it in Personal Growth Sessions and my 1-on-1 Employee Growth Training Sessions. The U. implies there are opposing forces around us at all times. You want to do what you want to do... and so does everyone else around you... therefore, we are bound to bump heads from time to time! As a leader, instead of attempting to control everything and everyone... what would happen if we decided to understand them and what they needed most? The two Evolving Questions are:

1. How do you understand this person? Why do you think they are the way they are? (your boss, employee/s, partner, kids, etc.)
2. What do you believe they need most from you RIGHT NOW?

If what they need line up with what you're willing to give... GREAT! If not, are you willing to meet their needs a little outside of your comfort zone; still doing and giving to the relationship what makes you feel good and mixing it with what they need? That's winning! What does your boss really need from you most RIGHT NOW? Your employees? Your partner? Etc.? As long as their need is in your boundary of ethical, respectful, and reasonable... meeting their deepest need raises your value; getting you closer to your dream!

R—Reveal

As I mentioned earlier, no one gets to lead healthy all the time. There are also no Crystal Balls that can tell you or other people what is going on in their personal lives. Sometimes, as a leader, it's healthier to reveal scars. If you are in a position of leadership... you know when you've been stressed (due to money, health, relationships, hurt, etc.) and haven't been your best, lead your best, or done your best! Revealing to your people that you're aware of your drop-off, accept full responsibility for it, explain why, and choosing to return to the leader you capable of; upholding previously set standards and expectations makes you human and an example of how H. U. R. T. Leadership is done!

Perhaps being honest with your boss, your coach, etc. about your hurt will breed empathy and enhanced connection. This does not imply expectations or standards will or should change, but an understanding of what's going on can go a long way!

T—Tough

Choosing to evolve in the face of hurt is tough. It's also going to require you learning some tough lessons about yourself. Hurt people hurt people... so chances are; if you've been hurt you most likely have said and done things professionally and personally that have hurt and negatively impacted those around you. Are you willing to accept responsibility for it, make amends, and accept your boss's, employee's, partner's, kid's feedback in a mature and evolved manner? Will you be able to give healthy, positive, tactful, and sincere feedback to someone else that needs it; allowing them to evolve, heal, and live their dream? That's toughness! Most people will either defend themselves or disconnect, some in the most extreme of ways! Leadership is not for the weak… it will take toughness to heal, lead, and evolve!

Learn from your hurt, choose to heal, understand your opposition, reveal instead of rebelling, and be tough in your process of leadership; making you the leader you are capable of and meant to be. Enjoy your evolution!!!

> *"Revealing to your people that you're aware of your drop-off, accepting full responsibility for it, explaining why, and choosing to return to the leader you're capable of; upholding previously set standards and expectations makes you human and an example of how H. U. R. T. Leadership is done!"*
> **– Andre Young**

WAY TO LEAD 6

A LEADER'S SELF-CARE

CHAPTER 39

Permission to Pause

We are all "Busy"... moving at the breakneck pace of our day, our job, our lives, and our Get-To's before and after work. Our "Busy" may look different from other people's "Busy", but it's always there! Although your "Busy" may make you successful, afford you the lifestyle you desire with a great paycheck, allow you to be the Mom or Dad of the year, or simply just allow you to make it through another day... The truth is, your "Busy" doesn't plan on stopping! It won't stop, until YOU decide to Stop it, Check It, and Change It! It's important to be careful... as the same "Busy" that brings you success, identity-fulfillment, or money will be the same "Busy" that engulfs you making you feel that it's all you are, erodes your relationships, and puts you in the ground due to stress! So, what to do?

Give yourself *Permission to Pause!* Yes... Permission to STOP your "Busy", Check your "Busy", and Change your "Busy"... if necessary. I don't mean a vacation! Vacations are nice... but may not always be what's needed. Especially, if you've been neglecting your partner, your kids, and your family due to your "Busy". It can feel like going on an expensive trip with strangers... and by the time you feel comfortable and adjusted, it's time to return... and let's face it... the coming back process is never as good as... or as exciting as the process of preparing to go! Then back to life you go, fearing the onslaught of emails, work, the house, and "Busy" is just laughing at you as it begins to slap you in the face again!

When I say Permission to Pause... I mean setting aside time regularly to sit without the noise of your life and either thinking or writing within these 3 categories:

Vision

What's your vision... your desired outcome and lifestyle in your 4 P's? It's not enough to just be great at one role; neglecting the others as if they don't matter or are less important. Could YOU imagine being treated as less important by your partner, your kids, your parents, or your job?

Working or Not?

Once you've clarified or re-clarified your vision. Are your daily actions, habits, and process helping you get there? It's easy to get "Busy" doing the things that need to be done. Are you doing things that are simply running the day-to-day operations of your job, your relationship, or family life or... can you adjust to a more efficient and smarter routine?

I do this once per month and call it... My "Get My Life Together Saturday!". My wife smiles as I occasionally tell her I need this day. I enjoy time in my office and go over all I am currently doing for my business, the kids, our relationship, and myself. Am I being "Busy" or "Better"? We'll delve more into this later in the book!

Continue/Stop/Start!

I enjoy this part of the Pause! *Continue*—You must be doing some great things to be where you are in life right now. Look around you... do you have shelter, people that enjoy you, not to mention... the ability to read this. Things could be a lot worse. So, continue what you are doing great!

Stop—What do you need to stop? We all engage in behaviors, whether as a Person, Professional, Partner, and Parent we can benefit from stopping. Let's STOP the unhelpful thought patterns and behaviors that are adding stress and leading to future chaos in our lives! If you can't stop them... at least be willing to modify and do them in moderation. Your future is counting on you!

Start—Although Stopping or Modifying the negatives in our lives is good... When we choose to start something new and replace it? This is the key to your Success, your Leadership, and your Work/Life Harmony! Many people interested in EVOLVING their lives tell me what they are willing to stop. As I mentioned, it's a good and motivated first step, but also an incomplete plan that is typically doomed to fail. The path is... Stopping something negative and substituting it with a reasonable and positive replacement behavior. So, what will you Continue, Stop, and Start in your 4 P's to become the leader you desire to be?

"Our "Busy" doesn't plan on stopping! It won't stop, until YOU decide to Stop it, Check It, and Change It!"
– Andre Young

CHAPTER 40

Managing Your Stress-Drip

We all have a Stress-Drip… "That thing" that's on the top of your pyramid that means the most to you in your life right now. That thing that would signify as your definition of success and has begun to identify who you are as a person. It may be being great at your job and earning that big income or title, or being the best mom or dad, or starting and maintaining your own business. Whatever it is… we all have it… and when we accompany "That Thing" with the time, energy, and daily brainpower it takes to stay successful; multiplied it by our "Get-To's" such as eating, doing the dishes, taking care of the kids, time for self-care, fun, etc… we have just turned on the ever-flowing Stress-Drip! As a leader focused on enhancing your Work/Life Harmony, the two important things to know is…

1. Whatever is on the top of your pyramid of success will drip down onto everything and everyone else you care about!

2. The Stress Drip will not stop… if fact it will only grow stronger; drowning YOU and your relationships from the inside. If you've had enough and are prepared, willing, and READY to do something about it! Here are the 4 Steps to Managing Your Stress-Drip!

Acknowledge

We must first acknowledge the positives of our Stress-Drip! The fact that you have a definition for your success, a plan, and are in current action-mode; making your dream happen makes you a remarkable individual! You're ahead of most, ambitions, and obviously dedicated to your goals and dreams! However, I will challenge you to evaluate and add to your definition of success. Many of us will deem ourselves successful because we've achieved or over-achieved in one specific area of our lives. You were an all-star athlete, achieved in business, hold an impressive title, and have most likely been this way ever since you can remember… but, you know that's no longer enough. What will you do to build and maintain a team of inspiring people around (personally and professionally) that add joy to your life!

Lastly, achieving and EVOLVING are two different things. Achieving can feel awesome but often signifies the job is done. EVOLVING is ongoing, fun, and satisfying for everyone! It's not about achieving the great role by YOUR standards. It's about EVOLVING in your roles by caring, asking, knowing, and being willing to meet the deepest needs of those around you and for yourself. If your idea of success is stressing you out and clashing with your life, home-life, and overall well-being… ACKNOWLEDGE where you are right now in life, ACCEPT it and stop trying to minimize and justify the effects of your stress, DECIDE what steps need to be taken in your daily life immediately and within the various roles you play, and start doing them NOW! That's leadership and how Work/Life Harmony is created!

Gratitude

A healthy dose of gratitude has never hurt anyone! As your Stress-Drip continues it will not matter how great a leader you are, how successful you are, how much money you make, how many awards you've won, or how many pats on the back you receive. Stress is stress and enough of it will make you feel like you are not enough, exhausted, on edge, drowning within yourself, and a worse version of yourself! Let gratitude help!

I often do seminars on "Got Gratitude?" and in them, I have the audience construct a list of 100 things they are grateful for. We then whittle away at that list down to their EVOLVING 3! What are the top three things you're grateful for (mine are love, health, and family)? Say them aloud! Are your current actions and daily words aligned with what you're most grateful for; allowing the good things in your life to continue and flourish? GRATITUDE and taking care of what really matters begins the process of shifting what's on the top of your pyramid!

Address & Apply

This is all about you and your needs.... YES, your needs matter! As a "Go-Getter", it's easy to pride yourself on how little rest you need, how much you can do, and what you've achieved. But, if you're reading this and it resonates with you... your other needs are SCREAMING! If you're a procrastinator and comfortable putting things off and this is resonating with you... your needs are SCREAMING; as YOU know you are capable of more and better!

ADDRESS... suggest you find out what your "real" needs are. Do you need rest, a vacation, a set or more organized schedule, to add something into your day, or take something out of your day? YOU know your patterns best... no excuses or rationalizations of why things can't change... what do you need to Continue/Stop/and Start in order to manage your Stress Drip? Believe it or not... your job, your partner, and this life WILL resume without you. Be sure to take care of yourself so you can be there for who and what really matters!

APPLY... tailors this process to YOU, who you are, and how quickly or slowly change is best for you. None of this will work unless you don't want to do it. People are people... and we are more willing to do what we want to do and what makes sense for us and our lifestyle. Address your Stress-Drip and tailor your plan to your lifestyle... as long as the direction is healthier, onward, and consistent!

EVOLVE. You are your patterns! Whatever you do daily and consistently you will get better at. What do your current patterns say about you as a Person, Professional, Partner, and Parent? If you like your answer... great... keep it up! If you don't... let's get started! Your EVOLUTION is a process... what you do when you finish this chapter and book is a choice... the first choice for your new and EVOLVED Life!

"Avoiding self-care, for even the noblest of reasons, will not only hurt you but eventually the ones you love"
– Andre Young

CHAPTER 41

Stop Drowning in 5

Water and I are not the best of friends and I've suffered several events of fear and panic related to water. While at the ocean... I remember a current slowly pulling me away from my friends and was lucky to have had a friend there to lend me a hand, but I will never forget how small I felt at that moment... how little people were aware of my stress and need. It was a surreal moment as I watched everyone having a great time while I was being swept away. Sounds a lot like life and leadership sometimes!

It may not be water; perhaps you're drowning as you struggle to keep a positive face and stiff chin as a leader at your job, maybe you're caring for an infant, your trying to manage an ever-increasing workload at your job, the after-school schedule of your kids, your marriage or relationship, or painfully not knowing what your next step is in life and thinking, "Is this it?".

Drowning is a draining experience as you feel scared, alone, and no one really knows the true amount of stress you're under. You can drown in your fears and failures; looking dejected and becoming apathetic… but also in your triumphs; trying to keep up with your success; always ready to accept more and feeling the pressure to always be looking "busy" and on top of your game. Either way, YOU are drowning and you'd like it to stop! At this point, you have choices:

1. You can succumb to the water in your life and accept your current existence; leaving you feeling miserable, resentful, and blaming everyone and everything.
2. You can find peace and purpose in your current life and lifestyle; making it tolerable as you settle into your life as it is.
3. Or… Try these 5!

Reset—It's easy to get caught in "Go" mode and feel as though if you STOP the world will stop spinning, chaos will ensue, and the sky will fall. Although you are important in YOUR world… It's amazing how others will tend to figure things out when you decide to stop or take a break. Believe me… your job existed before you and will run after you drop dead of a massive heart attack trying to be the world's best leader or employee… and… your partner existed before you and will live on after you dropped dead of a heart attack chasing your definition of success. I would hope the job and relationship are better with you… but you must know they have managed before you and will carry on without you! EVERYONE can make time for a few minutes, one hour (or a whole lot more) for reflection and resetting. While *RESETTING* ask yourself

- "What are all of the things I have to do?"
- "What am I doing and actually getting done?"
- "What's my real goal and end-game?"
- "Is what I'm doing working and beneficial to my life, relationships, and dream?"

- "Am I working smarter or am I working harder?"
- "What would be a smarter, healthier, and better way?"

Plan—Now you have the answer to these questions… it's time to plan! Whether you're achieving your goals, successful, and busy… or not achieving your goals, unsuccessful, and not busy… everyone needs these regular "Get Your Life Together Days!". This can take 30 minutes, and hour, or an afternoon.

- It's planning and writing down HOW you will work smarter and healthier to get to where you'd like to be in your 4 P's?
- What changes need to be made NOW?
- What your next moves will be?
- WHO can help and how?
- Writing your plan down and writing a To-Do List daily

Create Breaks—It's important to create a light at the end of the tunnel. We tend to work more steady, harder, and smarter when we know break-time or a vacation is coming. Get done what needs to get done… so you can relax, chill, and enjoy the fruits of your labor! As a leader, YOU have to know YOU. Some people are built to work and grind for days, weeks, or months on end with no break needed. Others are built to work and grind for a few hours and need a break. No judgment… you are you! Become aware of what you need and give yourself a break within reason. A break for me is as simple as taking a walk, a cigar, a date with my wife, throwing the ball with my kids… or as big as a scheduled family vacation. Whether big or small… If you don't plan to care for you… who will?

Love—Yes LOVE! I am not talking about the feeling of love… although awesome! I'm talking about "Doing" Love. Love is a verb… be sure you are actively loving the people around you: your partner, your children, your co-workers… and YOUSELF! It would be a shame to plan and work so hard for your success and desired lifestyle only to end up alone and lonely because you neglected the people that cared about you the most.

Treat Yourself—When you decide to stop drowning and work your 5... it can be easy to focus on the end. Realize... there is never an end to EVOLVING. Most people in positions of leadership will experience some sort of success and quickly move on to the next task or goal... either out of habit or a belief that the small wins are not that important. Only YOU know your list inside and out and what it takes to live YOUR dream... therefore, if you don't share or celebrate your successes... no one may know that they happened! So, be sure to treat yourself after successes... big and small! What do you do to treat yourself after success? What will you add to the list moving forward?

"Believe it or not... your job, your partner, and this life will resume without you. Be sure to take care of yourself so you can be there for who and what really matters!"
– Andre Young

CHAPTER 42

Superman / Superwoman
Syndrome

The demands of your day are numerous, constant, and at times thankless. If done well... it takes a special person to do what you do... and accomplish what you accomplish in a day. You are SUPER, but you may not need to be Superman or Superwoman.

So often; throughout my life, my years as a marriage counselor, as Founder of You Evolving Now, and as a person... I have seen men and women assume the role of Superman or Superwoman only to spiral and burnout into the abyss of resentment and frustration. You may have taken this role out of necessity; being a single parent or some other unfortunate situation. However, most of the time, people assume the role and take on work and household tasks out of initial kindness, strength, ability, control issues, or lack of other options. Remember... The problem eventually becomes... what you start and allow in the beginning, will be expected in the end!

If you have accepted too many tasks out of kindness... resentment can begin to creep into your day-to-day as it becomes expected you will continue the tasks forever; making it necessary for you to communicate you do not want your kindness taken for granted, as a weakness, or as a convenience.

If you have become Superman or Superwoman due to strength of ability... take it as a compliment; making it necessary for you to improve your teaching skills; allowing others to learn the same skill set. If you are completing tasks because it's easier for you to do them rather than teaching someone... your resentment is your fault!

Some assume the role of Superman or Superwoman because if anyone else does the task... they'll foul it up. Sound familiar? The fact they may "foul it up" may be true... but YOU having the control issue is also true! The only way others will learn and be able to assist is to jump in, make mistakes, and make the process somewhat their own. This is hard to accomplish while being judged, put-down, and under-valued. It may not be done your way, but it's done and you didn't have to do it. I understand this new way will cause you great anxiety... but so does a bad work environment and failing relationship!

Lack of option is a legitimate argument and leaves many leaders and single parents/caregivers in a quandary; making it necessary to elicit help from friends, neighbors, co-workers, the community, and your kids. You don't t have to go at it alone... unless you choose to. Most people are willing to help, but it will take you being humble enough to connect, explain, and ask for help!

Every superhero takes solace in their alter ego. Superman sometimes gets to escape the pressure of being the hero when he is Clark Kent. Clark Kent gets to take a breath, go on vacation, see the world through a different lens, experience the same people in his day-to-day in a different light. In a world always urging you to be super, move forward, and succeed... today... I encourage you to embrace your Clark Kent, put your cape down, and allow other people to be a hero!

"What you start and allow in the beginning, will be expected in the end... Be Mindful!"

– Andre Young

CHAPTER 43

Success... Now What?

Success; another amazing word, feeling, and experience! Most of us are chasing it and on a continual uphill climb to achieve it. Regardless of our different definitions of success... we all have one, but what happens when we make it up Success Mountain... Then what?

Many decide to relax and coast, but leaders know nothing stays the same for long. Some get bored, depressed, lazy... and perhaps the success you dreamed of isn't what you thought it would be or feel like. So, what the heck do you do when you've achieved your success? do?

Take Care of Who or What has taken care of you.

On your climb to success there have been many people who have supported your ascent; some directly, some indirectly, some positively, and some with their negativity and doubt. Your partner who supported, maybe not always like you wanted ... but supported your time away, your dedication to the grind, caring for the things you didn't make and take the time to do. Your kids who missed you and watch you choose your grind and definition of success over their playtime, sporting games, etc. I could go on… but you get where I'm going! I equate it to your car… your car is your everything and without it… you'd struggle to get to work and places you enjoy.

If you don't put gas in it and at the least the basic oil change… your car will stop running, your life will get WAY more difficult, and you will only have yourself to blame! Think about it… you would have to ignore the gas gauge on your dashboard, the engine light, and the oil light that would be blinking and screaming for your attention to get to that point. Your car told you what was needed and when it was needed… and you ignored it; just like you may be ignoring your employee, your employer, your significant other, and your kids. Whether it's by their words, actions, or inaction… they're communicating and it's your job as a leader to decipher the message. Be sure to take care of who and what has taken care of you during and after your climb up Success Mountain! What does "Take Care of" mean?

Tip: EVOLVE your leadership by marrying what you'd like to do for your people with what your people actually want and need from you.

Expand Your Vision and Your Craft

You've made it to the top of your Success Mountain and the view has broadened and expanded… has your vision? The view climbing uphill may have been very singularly focused and full of grit and grind. But, becoming successful and staying successful are two different things and now that you've made it… I assume you'd like to keep it! The best way to do that is to continue learning your craft; whether your desired craft is as a business owner, boss, parent, partner, etc. Learn more about it! Be curious about your passion, the people involved in it, and how to best move forward and expand!

We must expand our knowledge and work to anticipate what the upcoming changes are; planning how to best prepare and adjust. Example: you have been successful in business, but the trend is changing and what's working now will not provide the same results in the future... get ahead of this or become Blockbuster Video! Your kids are becoming teenagers or preparing to leave the house... now what?

One way to ensure the expansion of your vision and craft is to reach out and connect with like-minded leaders with the same grit and passion as you. It's not necessary they be in the same line of work... just the same type of passion, grit, and onward march towards success. When you're with them and after leaving them (whether a call, video meeting, or in-person) do you feel motivated, inspired, excited, and idea-filled? If yes... that's growth and EVOLUTION!... and the people to be sure to spend more time with! If not... it's time to add to your team!

If the excuse is, "I don't know of anyone like that", that's what networking and social media are for. Join networking groups in and outside of your immediate area and follow inspirational and successful people or groups via LinkedIn, Facebook, and Instagram. Reach out, comment, and *connect*. You'd be surprised what will happen!

If you desire to expand socially; not professionally... there are awesome sites that are interest-based. If you like to juggle; there are groups out there for jugglers... and they meet often! An example is www.meetup.com If you like dining out, books, movies, business... there are groups (some free) just for you and sometimes designated for your target age range! Expand, connect, and EVOLVE!

The Behind the Scenes Grind

Very few people will ever fully see or respect what it took for you to accomplish your definition of success or the success: the late nights, the arguments, exhaustion, the joy, and sometimes the despair. The grind it took for you to achieve your initial success must continue... however, it may look different. The fact you chose to grind your way up Success Mountain says a lot about you and it's unlikely you're not the type to relax for too long; so let's start building and leading other leaders! Perhaps in developing new hires, new content, consulting, mentoring... the goal here is to create; all with the purpose of maintaining your success, legacy, and on-going impact and evolution!

Self-Care

For many Success Mountain Climbers... self-care doesn't come easy! You are most likely use to resting when you absolutely know you need to or crash because your mind and body are shot. Self-Care is essential to living your best and most evolved lifestyle. Create time for health and wellness whether its gym time, yoga, a walk, or something that involves movement and healthier consumption. There's no sense in being successful if you are at constant threat of dying of a heart attack, neglecting loved-ones, or engaging in addiction to decompress! Make Time & Take Time to be with friends... Remember those people? Those people who enjoy you for YOU... not your success! Give yourself permission to chill... guilt-free for a while!

Freedom was the ultimate reason you've worked this hard and climbed Success Mountain... it's time to enjoy it! My wife was recently home sick from work; that's not the good part, but as she laid in the bed... I was honored to be able to care for her. I worked from home that week in my office and ventured upstairs often to check on her and said to myself... I have worked this hard and created a lifestyle for myself and our family that I can lay with her and watch a movie mid-day. If I were an employee and someone said, "Want to watch this movie mid-day and it's ok with the boss"... I'd jump at the chance. So why not? Make yourself and those who have taken care of you more of a priority and give yourself permission to take advantage of the success you've created!

"Your success is only as good as your process!"
– Andre Young

CHAPTER 44

Are You "Burnt-Out" or "Bored-Out"?

I'm sure you've heard the term, "Burnt-Out". It's a hard thing to watch someone you know go through and an even harder thing to experience ourselves; especially as leaders; because everyone is always watching... and judging! In all jobs, teams, or relationships there can easily come a time when Burn-Out seeps in. In starts ever-so-slowly, sneaks into our jobs, duties, and/or relationships and BOOM... we feel instantly miserable, fed-up, unappreciated, and the list goes on! Today, I want to share the difference between "Burnt-Out" and "Bored-Out"; they're different and will require different courses of action.

Burn-Out typically occurs to someone who was initially "All-In", motivated, inspired, and capable. However, along the way, things changed... perhaps life circumstances, poor management in the company, change in management, or... things stayed exactly the same and the holes in the system or relationship became more evident and their voice was not heard or respected; allowing the day-to-day grind to make them more bitter than better. Burn-Out tends to deal with a former good or awesome person, partner, or employee now suffering from a righteous ego; becoming a silent negative force or an actively disruptive cog to the flow of things.

"Bored-Out" refers to a person, partner, teammate, or employee that has resorted to droning about. This person may be productive regarding their expected duties, but have lost their vigor and are silently unhappy. Magnify this over months, years, and decades... can you imagine the culture in your business, your team, and uuuhhhggg... your relationship! This person may believe they are capable of more, but has not asserted themselves to ask for more or to do more... for various reasons. Perhaps they haven't seen more, or know there's a possibility for more. Perhaps they don't believe in themselves or scared to fail or succeed.

Typically, many people are unaware of what all of their options are and opportunities have not been presented as realistic for their future! This individual may constantly be looking for a way out... and anyone constantly ready to swipe left of their job and in their relationship cannot give you their all! So, what to do?

If you are "Burnt-Out":

1. Remember your "Why". In my seminars, I often discuss marrying Yourself, your Dream, and your "Why". Why did you start in the job you're in, the sport you play, the relationship you're in? Although things have changed; there's value in remembering the beginning! What you really enjoyed and enjoy about that job, that sport, or that relationship... because "That Thing" is still there. Although I'm no longer a Mental Health Therapist, I never stopped liking to help people, listening to people, connecting, problem-solving, and being positive.

   Through the rough times in relationships; remember your "Why" and who your partner, friend, children, etc. really are. It's still in there. Although, you cannot recreate what was... you can choose to rebuild on the foundation of your "Why"! So, remember your "Why" and get back to being a leader!

2. Maximize the positives of the job, the team, the relationship and enjoy! Everything has its negatives and positives… what are they and be sure to Make Time and Take Time to appreciate the positives and enjoy them!

3. Enjoy the relationships and the people around you. There are so many people you encounter on the daily tour of your life as a person, at your job, or as a teammate… from the person you get your coffee from, co-workers, etc.… find joy in their conversation, get to know them, create friendships, and have fun in working together. The mundane task in your day "is what it is"… can you create joy in how it's done?

4. Recognize and maximize your skillset and superpower, communicate your concerns with decision-makers in a positive manner, and find a way to make an impact with what you do great! The worse they can say is no. Leaders are always creating opportunities to increase their value!

5. If none of this is for you, you can't get back to you, happy, content, or be joyful where you are… perhaps it's life's way of telling you "It's Time". Time to move on, take what you've learned, accept what you did great, good, and bad; along with what the company, team, or relationship did great, good, and bad… and impart all of your new-found wisdom somewhere else.

If your "Bored-Out":

1. DO your best and BE your best. This will be number one and three… as I'll explain. Do the things you've agreed to do and do it to the best of your ability. "Be your best" means to be the best person you can be: positive, willing, caring, inspiring, and don't forget to smile!

2. Communicate with decision-makers, leaders, or with the people you care about in relationships that you are bored or interested in attempting more things Explain what exactly that means for you, ask if there's more to do, and share your ideas. It may sound like, "I appreciate being here. I feel I have more to offer and am excited to do and be more here. Is there more I can do? I'd like to learn or try _____. What would I have to do to make that happen?" I don't promise you'll always get what you want, but you've been heard. If you get it, great! If you don't… you'll need to understand their "Why" and you'll eventually have a decision to make. The focus here is to communicate, be willing, stay positive, and ALWAYS be ready!

3. Do and Be your best… we're back… and this is ONLY for jobs and teams! Why…because we can't ask for more or different responsibilities and stink at the ones we are currently doing. That's crazy! Can you imagine someone saying their bored at their job, but are currently inefficient and messing everything up; only to ask for something more or different? Our response would typically be… "Do this right first!". Not to say it's right, but it is the typical response. The truth is… the current task may not be that individual's superpower and they may surprise you as they venture to a new and different task or position. A great leader doesn't try to fit a square peg in a round hole. But remember, at your job or on your team, if you're the one that wants more, you must be the one doing and being your best first!

4. Maximize relationships and enjoy the people in your daily space. Get unbored by enjoying others and dismissing the daily negative complaining and gossip. Find the positive people and create a new experience in the space you choose to be!

5. If none of this is for you, you can't get back to you, happy, content, or joyful… perhaps it's life's way of telling you "It's Time". Time to move on, take what you've learned, accept what

you did great, good, and bad; along with what the company, team, or relationship did great, good, and bad... and impart your new-found wisdom somewhere else.

I hope this shed light on the difference between "Burnt-Out and Bored-Out" and how to navigate these tough times. It can happen to the best of us. Remember, Work/Life Harmony matters... putting your head down and droning has never fixed a problem.

"Passivity in your life will not excuse you from consequences; get active in living your best life and enjoy!"
– Andre Young

WAY TO LEAD 7
THE LEADER'S 7

CHAPTER 45

The Leader's 7

This here is the cherry on top of leadership! In reading this book; you've learned how to prepare for leadership, get your confidence up, enhance your gratitude, do leadership daily, how to take risks, and how to really do self-care! Now, with the Leader's 7, you get to become multi-lingual and possess the ability to speak everyone's language that is following your lead!

A quick question, if you planned to move to France and live there for the rest of your life, would you learn French? Why? You could get along without learning the language; but your ability to connect, feel comfortable, and your overall experience would be limited. Learning the language of the land opens us up to better communicate... and from the most important leadership perspective... enhance our ability to understand and meet the needs of the people we're leading!

There are seven languages employees, athletes, students, and our followers want to hear, need to hear, and benefit most from hearing from their leaders that impact motivation, inspiration, self-worth, bonding, and purpose! At times, in this section, you'll hear me refer to those we lead as Followers. This is not meant to be a slight or disrespect. Unfortunately, as much as we value leadership, being in control, having the title of Boss, and all of the glory that goes with fancy titles; we, in contrast, view following or being a follower with an equal amount of disdain. Shouldn't that judgment depend on who and why someone chooses to follow? No one knows it all and hopefully you will surround yourself with people that know more than you do in certain areas... it's how you level up!

At some point, in all areas of our life... we must know when it's best to follow until we can lead. True leadership is synonymous with mentoring and allowing others to emerge into leaders themselves!

As leaders... we need to be able and willing to speak all 7 Languages, but each of your people have a top one or two that are most important, meaningful, inspiring, and influencing to them. Once you know their top one or two... you're now able to speak their language and make an impact! Also, once you know... you can't unknow and it would be a cold-hearted choice to know what language would best make an impact for a person and choose not to speak it!

Your self-awareness as a leader is as important as being aware of others; therefore, it's equally necessary for you to know what your top two languages are... as you will bond most easily with those that share that same language. Also, which two resonate the least with you... as you may struggle the most with the people who prefer those languages. Understanding this concept transforms someone you'd typically describe as frustrating, annoying, not a team player, opinionated, insubordinate, and a few other choice words I'm sure you've said in your mind into someone that simply speaks a different language... and now you'll know how to approach!

In this Leader's 7 section, you will learn the 5 Types of Employees / Athletes / Students, The 7 Languages, The Most Powerful Preface Statement in the World, The Positive-Sandwich, and how to speak The

7 in casual conversation… and in those "tough conversations" leaders would prefer not to have, but are necessary to maintain the vision, direction, accountability, and process for success!

"True leadership is synonymous with mentoring and allowing others to emerge into leaders; allowing evolution to take its course with us not having to demand the credit!"

– Andre Young

CHAPTER 46

The 5 Types

Whether in big fancy white-collar corporate offices, the bluest of blue-collar jobs, professional teams, to pick-up games, to students… The same 5 Types exist in every group! Knowing their type won't help you speak The Leader's 7 Language per se (only asking will do that), but once we know what type someone is… we know more of what to expect; allowing us to realistically understand who we're engaging with and what kind of effort we'll need to expend to satisfy the expectations of our vision.

Many times, as leaders we enter relationships and conversations with a "Should Mentality". We know what we know, have done our job for a while, can spit out all the acronyms of our job and training, believe that everyone wants to move up and cares about the job and vision like we do… and we live in the world of "Should"!

Well, it would be nice if everyone knew what you knew, saw the bigger picture, and cared like you cared… it would make life a whole lot easier! However, that's not always the case. Knowing the 5 Types, which type your people are, and the language they will most benefit from... will help to remove your "Leadership Shoulds"; enhancing your understanding, empathy, and a realistic plan of how to move forward in a more positive and productive manner. So, what are the 5 Types?

The Inspired & Motivated

Don't we all wish we had a team full of "The Inspired & Motivated"! The individual who is genuinely happy to be at the job and on the team. They are positive, ready, willing, motivated, and... CONSISTENTLY CAPABLE! They also leave you in awe due to the amount of potential they have leftover to grow. "The Inspired & Motivated" have goals, have drive, and you can see it and feel it when you're around them.

Years ago, when I hired staff for You Evolving Now... I hired based on the look in a person's eyes. The way they looked at me when I spoke. When you're speaking to or teaching "The Inspired & Motivated" their eyes are big, they blink less, and you can actually see their eyes widen as you watch your words, concepts, and reasoning funnel into their eyes like vacuums. I know, it sounds weird and maybe a little disgusting, but it's true!

Note: The key to the Inspired & Motivated will be to learn their Leader's 7 Language and speak it to them often. This will be the first key for all 5 Types, but the "Inspired & Motivated will tend to produce the most on a consistent basis... making your company or team thrive! Secondly, find out their dream, their passion, and their "Why" and see if you can be of service. Perhaps their dream is to move up in the organization or something that directly benefits you and the company or team... If so, great! If not; and their dream is something unrelated and you assist anyway... their appreciation, multiplied by their existing great effort can only be a bonus to you and the organization! In addition, you did something awesome for someone else... and that's leadership!

Notice, I did not mention the "L-Word"... Loyalty. No one owes a leader loyalty and in this Swipe-Left Generation... people get jobs, leave jobs, move, advance, etc. Just because you want "Inspired & Motivated" to stay for thirty or forty years... doesn't mean it's going to happen and they certainly don't owe it! Be mindful of that "L-Word"! Treat the "Inspired & Motivated" well and perhaps they will stay or at the least are willing to help you find and train their replacement when the time comes to leave.

If you are the "Inspired & Motivated" be sure to ask the "Get-Great Question"! All 5 Types are encouraged to ask, but I know you will follow through and do it! It sounds like this... "I want to be great here, the best! Can you help me? What do I need to know and do to____ (insert dream/goal) _____? Then... be quiet, listen, and apply!

Is the answer shared with you reasonable, doable, and fair for you, who you are, and the LIFESTYLE you want? If so, great... do what was asked and start by doing it a little out of your comfort zone. It's important not to dive in the rabbit hole so far that you lose yourself, your relationships, self-respect, and your Work/Life Harmony... leading to resentment, frustration, and bitterness. And remember, what's done in the beginning... will become expected in the middle and in the end! Be mindful and careful not to let your EXTRA be taken for granted or undervalued. We all have to pay our dues in the beginning; however, as a leader... you will most likely have to protect "The Inspired & Motivated" from themselves and the politics of the company and team. It's easy to ask and EXPECT the person that is already doing more, great at their job, and most apt to say "Yes" to continue doing more... on and off work hours, lunch breaks, late-night emails, and everyone else's work. Protecting "The Inspired & Motivated" from Burn-Out will be an essential part of maintaining, growing, and evolving your team!

Lastly, never let a job or relationship make you become less of what you are and who you are... I call this the Less/More Leadership Rule! Always DO and BE your best... regardless of the treatment you're receiving and regardless of the others around you (co-workers, teammates, students, friends, and even family) that have decided to stop working hard, be less, and do less.

The time will come... YOUR TIME WILL COME... when you have stayed great long enough that you will either be rewarded for your worth, go elsewhere for your worth, or create your own worth! That cannot happen if you've decided to be less due to frustration and personal protest. Think of a star-athlete... they are unhappy with the team they're on, their coaching, their pay, losing all the time, or all of the above. They may hold-out... but the worse thing they can do is play to less of their ability. They lose all leverage against the team they are on and the other teams that may be interested in the very near future. Be mindful not to lose your leverage by choosing to BE or DO less!

New & Unknown

"New & Unknown is exactly what it sounds like. The person is new to the job, team, or school and we know nothing about them except their name, what's on paper, and what they say. They will be this Type for a while, some longer or shorter than others. There is a great positive and negative here! The positive is... eventually, this person will show their true selves regarding their personality; but their behavior, actions, and work habits will also be dictated by the culture of your organization! If your culture is good, promotes the values of your mission statement and vision, and you have other leaders that maintain that gold-star standard... this person tends to be just fine. If culture not is not that way... you're going to have to start hoping, praying, or upping your leadership to usher them into new culture!

Note: Typically, people that are new will want to continue doing what they were initially trained to do. This is people! Therefore... it's important how "The New & Unknown" are trained, asking the Leader's Questions, and leading with expectations. If people don't know what the expectations are, and what the consequences are when expectations are ignored... how can progress and success happen?

If you are the "New & Unknown", be mindful of the first new co-workers, teammates, or students you meet. Too many times, people stay with the first group of people they met or are trained by. Perhaps out of a sense of comfortability, laziness to meet others, shyness... whatever it is... be mindful; as it's always amazed how quickly people can get comfortable. If the first group of people you meet are positive, motivated, inspired, have bigger goals than yours, are about doing life and the job right, not just getting it done, and BONUS... can do it with a smile... then stay with that person or group! If they are negative, gossipers, short-cutters, and have no aspirations inside or outside of work... I implore you to expand your circle right away! Notice... I didn't say cut them... The negative gossiper with little aspirations CAN BE a nice person to you, funny, and entertaining.... just not where you spend the bulk of your time.

YOU stay positive, motivated, learning, and advancing in your life and watch who stays around or comes back around when they are ready to evolve!

The Steady Stream

"Steady Streams" are important people to any company or team. They are not the raging river like the "Inspired & Motivated", but how many people are? Remember, steady streams fill up those raging rivers! This is the person you can count on to produce the same level of work... rain, sleet, or snow. They are dependable and know their job. If you asked the "Inspired & Motivated" who they trust... this tends to be who they say! This is the worker that puts their head down and gets things done, is always there, and doesn't seem to expect much or make many waves. You've even considered them for a promotion or moving them up to first string. At times, they show that spark you really desire, but truthfully... they are content right where they are... and that's ok!

Note: I love meeting with employees and athletes on-site for my 1-on-1 Growth Training Sessions; what an honor to work with companies and teams gets it and are willing to impact their people in all roles they play. One day, I met with a man named Carl (not his real name) and he was awesome! He was funny, came to work every day, did great work, was dependable, and said all of the things a supervisor would say. He was very captivating; so, I asked had he ever thought of a leadership position. Without skipping a beat, he replied "Oh No, I just want to come to work and do my job. This is the best job I've ever had and I'm good!". This man was happy, content, and didn't want to be "bothered" by increased expectations, headaches, emails, etc. He was the "Steady Steam"!

Be mindful, not everyone may want your definition of "More", "Success", or what comes along with advancing. Every company and team need its first-string all-stars, talented second-string, and so on. Being willing to treat "Steady Streams" with the same respect and vigor… it will say a lot about your leadership!

The Here, but Not Here

The "Here, but Not Here" can prove to be your most frustrating. Not because they are negative, but because you don't know if they're staying or going. Just like with anything, they're positives and negatives. People can be different Types at different times, based on life circumstances, where they are in their careers, and many other reasons. In my last stint as an employee… I was the positive version of "Here, but Not Here".

I had my business, You Evolving Now, up and running, and ready to take off. I knew it was about to hit and make major impacts; leading to more money and less time available to work a full-time job during the traditional work-week. However, my wife and I decided to build a house. If you've ever been through that process, you know the ending price is never what you initially agreed to… and then you have to furnish it! So, I needed a job.

I wanted a job that was somewhat flexible, I didn't want promotions, or a lot of responsibly, because I had so much to do running a business, having three kids at the time (now four), and working a job. I entered job interviews eager and nervous all at the same time, because I was married to my dream (my business) and was determined for them to know… I'm capable of what I was applying for, eager to start, and needed the job. It was equally important for me they knew I was a speaker, author, and Founder of my own company. Pretty much saying... I'm Here, but Not Here and preferably... not here for long! But, while I'm here... I'm going to give you all I have, be a great person, a great influencer, and do a great job; but anything out of work hours... I cannot do.

Luckily, they hired me and 8 months later, I was gone and living my dream! Although, they knew I was leaving... and I was doing everything to not make myself the fool and be there for years. I like to think, both the job and I made out for the better for having each other! However, I didn't take away their stress of, "When's he leaving?", "How and when do we start looking for someone to replace him?", and so many other thoughts of that nature.

The negative side of the "Here, but Not Here" coworker, employee, or teammate is the opposite. They are there... we can't deny their body is there and they're standing right in front of us... but they are miserable, apathetic, complaining, slow to work, quick to do anything else but work, and may a part of creating the negative culture that is killing the vibe of your organization and swallowing up so many "New & Unknowns" along the way!

Note: A BIG Thank You to the company that hired me when I was "Here, but Not Here". Thank You for taking a chance, believing in my dream, asking about my progress, teaching me the job, and being happy for my success! If you are a company or team... could you and will you do the same? The truth is... they got a good worker that was eager to make a great impact in the community (I was a member of a Mental Health Team; working with the most severe population of those suffering from Schizophrenia and Psychotic Disorders). They could have done a lot worse... and so could I! As a leader, what win-win situations will you begin to create for your people?

If you're the Negative "Here, but Not Here" and you're looking at your job or team as JUST a "job" or a stepping stone... that's fine. Let it be what it is, but it benefits you tremendously to take it for what it is and what the opportunity can offer. Remember "Why" you are there, what you can learn from it, and that your reputation will follow you. It's your reputation on the line… and it's pretty ugly if you can only act positive when things are going 100% your way. Personal Leadership implies you are your best self throughout the journey, not just when you get to your desired destination.

Lastly, knowing their Leader's 7 Language may be just enough to get the "Here, But Not Here" over the hump to either their dream and being positive because they know you care enough to support their real dream, purpose, and superpower. People who get to talk about their dream and show it off tend to be happier people… and happier people tend to work harder and better for you!

The Grouch

Remember Oscar the Grouch from Sesame Street? This is your "Grouch", just without the green-haired suit… I hope! This person is typically miserable and would rather be anywhere but at job or on the team. The first key is… understanding their "Why". Did you bring them into the organization this way? Did they just get this way or was it a slow burn? Has something happened in their personal life? What? Perhaps, we can find understanding and empathy in their "Why"… maybe we can't.

The second key is, after understanding and doing your best to assist; we must make clear expectations of what needs to be done and how it's expected to get done to move positively toward the vision of success. This mixture allows you to maintain empathy, but not so much that their behavior and attitude is allowed to continue and have a hand in destroying your desired culture.

I learned this concept I just mentioned when I was an employee. I often speak to corporations and teams about "How to Manage C.H.A.N.G.E." and one of the ways is developing Employee Leadership, because anyone at any position can be a leader if they chose to be! It's all about how a person chooses to carry themselves throughout the day, the words they choose to use throughout the day, and making a decision to build rather than destroy. I was intent on being that when I was an employee… and I can specifically remember a co-worker at the time that was not. She was a very thin older woman, always amazingly dressed, and formerly worked as a big-time executive, but now presented as miserable, complaining all the time, and often sat on a chair looking as if she were dying. It was uncomfortable to be around, to hear, and to witness day in and day out.

One day, I politely asked her "Why do you work here… you don't seem to like it very much?". Her answer almost knocked me out of my chair and it very suddenly put everything into a new perspective.

She mentioned she needed to show up every day to maintain Healthcare; as she had a life-threatening condition. She was struggling with a mass in her body that weighed almost as much as she did and caused her intense pain most of the time. Therefore, she had to come to work feeling like death to maintain her insurance so she could receive treatment, so she wouldn't die! Now… That's working for a living! I immediately understood why she spoke the way she spoke and why her mood was what it was! Some people call off when they have the sniffles… she came to work while actually dying.

Note: This scenario above, doesn't waive employee, co-worker, or teammate obligation of expectations and leadership… it simply illuminates the power of staying curious and asking "Why". This question tends to only be asked upon being "New & Unknown". Let's not forget to ask again and again to our existing people… as their "Why" can and will change over time!

These are The 5 Types: The Inspired & Motivated, The New & Unknown, The Steady Stream, The Here, but Not Here, and The Grouch! Now you know the 5 Types, which one are your people? Which one are you? What did you take from this chapter to help you positively impact your team, mission, and culture moving forward?

"The time will come… YOUR TIME WILL COME… when you have stayed great long enough that you will either be rewarded for your worth, go elsewhere for your worth, or create your own worth!

That cannot happen if you've decided to BE and DO less due to frustration and personal protest."
– Andre Young

CHAPTER 47

The World's Best
Preface Statement

Now that you know the concept of The Leader's 7 and The 5 Types...
Let's take a second to learn The World's Best Preface Statement;
preparing you and for success as a leader when it's time to have that
"tough conversation" with your employee, player, student, kids, or
even your partner. I define success as a mixture of creating the highest
probable situation in which understanding, empathy, and focus on the
overall evolution for both sides are highest... mixed with your ability to
put your head on your pillow at night in peace; knowing you positively
addressed significant situations!

I began using this Preface Statement in my former career of 19 years
as a Mental Health Therapist and found it made difficult conversations
much easier and life-changing for both myself... and my clients! So,
what is it and how do you do it?

When someone was new to therapy, I wanted to know as much about their "Why" as possible. Their experience with other therapists, what they wanted to get out of the experience of sitting with me, if they wanted to change... or not, and how they knew therapy would be working. This quickly allowed for bonding and increased understanding and a plan of how to work together. Ending this process, I always stated and asked the World's Best Preface Statement... *"I'm excited we're going to be working together; at some point I may have to say something that's hard for you to hear and I wouldn't be doing my job if I didn't. Is that going to be OK?".*

This question has batted 1000%... as the person responds "Yes" and we begin the process! The Preface Statement may not be used for a month or six months, but as a leader... you know, at some point, the time will come that a hard conversation will be necessary... and now you'll be prepared for it! At some point your client, employee, student, etc. are going to say or do something that as a leader you MUST challenge. If, as leaders, you do not... it is as much your fault that chaos ensues! In a company and on a team... people are watching and it doesn't take long for people to test and know that the boundaries you've set are bull crap! So, what's next?

Now it's time to confront... take a deep breath... remember, you've already set this up a while ago! This may happen in mid-conversation or a planned meeting... and it sounds like this... *"Remember when I said there may come a time when I have to say something that may be hard for you to hear?".* They will either say "Yes" or nod their head. You say, *"Are you ready?".* In my experience, people tend to smirk, smile, or even chuckle... but they all have taken a deep breath and you can see them emotionally and physically brace themselves for impact. Now you have the green light to say what needs to be said. Remember, this works best if we've applied the concepts of The 7 Ways to Lead discussed throughout this book! People are more willing to accept feedback from someone they enjoy, trust, and respect. However, the Preface Statement doesn't stop there. How we discuss the issue matters.

1. When you say, "Are you ready?" and they give the nod of acceptance... simply saying the issue, your concern, and what can be done to correct it may work for the some, but not for all.
2. EVOLVE the conversation by using my Positive Sandwich! This will allow for understanding, empathy, brainstorming, and planning... allowing them increased self-awareness and ownership of their new direction!

The Positive Sandwich in its simplest form is starting your constructive criticism or problem-solving inquiry with a positive about the individual's work or effort. Then, dive into the issue; using the power of questions. Ending with a positive, a "Thank You", and a plan with expectations and willingness to move forward and evolve!

The Positive Sandwich may sound like this... "Hi Scott (completely made up name), Remember that time I said I might have something to say that would hard for you to here"? "Are you ready?". "We love having you and you've been doing a great job when you're here; can you help me to understand why you're coming in late so often? Perhaps the team or myself and be of help; what do you think is the best way to fix this and move forward?".

You will learn a lot about Scott in the next few minutes! If what the person says is reasonable, doable, and fair... great! If not... is their room for compromise, change, or perhaps this isn't the job or team for them. Lastly, "Scott, thanks for meeting with me and making this an easier conversation. So, moving forward... the plan is to _____. Awesome! If you have any questions or need anything, let me know. Have a great day!".

Stay tuned in the next chapters for the advanced version of The Positive Sandwich; as we include their Leader's 7 Language to make this even more personal and impactful! Speaking a person's desired language will attract their ear, their attention, and their curiosity... allowing you to be viewed as helpful as opposed to demeaning and demanding. So how does that Preface Statement go so far:

Pre-Issue

You: *"I'm excited we're going to be working together and I know you're going to do great; at some point, I may have to say something that's hard for you to hear and I wouldn't be doing my job if I didn't. Is that going to be OK?".*

Person: "Yes"

Issue needs to be addressed

You: *"Hi_____, Remember when I said there may come a time when I have to say something that may be hard for you to hear?".*

Person: *"Yes" or nod of the head*

You: *"Are you ready?".*

Person: *Usually a deep breath and brace for impact moment*

You: *Use the Positive sandwich!*

CHAPTER 48

The Leader's 7 Languages

Now that The Leader's 7 concept, the 5 Types, and the World's Best Preface Statement is under your belt... it's time for the 7 Languages your employees, teams, athletes, or students want to hear, need to hear, and benefit most from hearing; allowing increased motivation, inspiration, sense of belonging, and culture enhancement! Remember, everyone likes all seven and it's our job as leaders to be able to speak all seven; but each of your people have a top one or two! So, what are the Languages:

1. *Goodies Time*
2. *Quality Minutes*
3. *Recognition & Affirmation*
4. *Knowledge & Advancement*
5. *Incentives*

6. *Flexibility*
7. *Respect*

Goodies Time

Some individuals on your team will love the "Goodies" the job or team provides. Yes, I'm referring to the doughnuts and coffee in the morning, the pizza and other goodies provided for lunch, etc.! Although, this is not one of my top two languages… I must admit, I stayed at a job a few months longer than I should have because their "Goodie Time" was off the charts! Lunch was usually catered by various pharmaceutical reps and the spread was like having a gourmet dinner for lunch almost every day. I still think about it and… Wow!!!

I'm not suggesting this type of spread for your people; however, it's important for you to know this is someone's Language. A treat to coffee or something small can go a long way. Recognizing the hectic mornings of most people, the power of them not having to reach into their pocket to pay, and the human nature of people to socialize over a meal or drink can be priceless!

I once had a boss enter the office and announced an impromptu road trip for our small staff of four. It was a beautiful day; we walked to a café down the street and she treated us to coffee. Something so small still sticks out in my mind as we/I were able to get out of the office, do something different, enjoy the sunshine, and a cup of coffee together; conversing about nonwork-related topics… Small but BIG! Note: Many companies, teams, and you may do this regularly… be sure as the leader to partake with your people; investing socially in the experience… not just providing it!

Quality Minutes

Some of your workers, athletes, and students value YOUR time. I remember so many times in which the figure-head of the team I played for or company I worked for were so busy being busy that I and others became a non-entity; simply slaving away unnoticed and underappreciated. The same coach that recruited me to play college football didn't say another word to me in the hallways over my next five years. (Yes, I said five years, Lol!) CEOs pass you in the hallway with head and eyes down; as everyone attends to their robotic mission of doing their part for the company. ENOUGH!!!

Some of your people value their leader taking a few minutes to speak with them about other things than just the job. For example: "Hi _____, how was your weekend", "What are your plans for your weekend?", "What are your plans for the summer?", "How was your evening?", "How's your family doing with _____" (this assumes you care enough as a leader to know about our worker's, student's or player's life and family)... are their kids into sports, dance, acting, etc.? What are the hobbies and passions of your people outside of the job?

Quality Minutes doesn't suggest you devote an hour to each worker or individual, but simply being mindful to use the person's name while asking unnecessary, but powerful questions will go a long way to the person who enjoys this Language. It also benefits the culture as it creates and enhances curiosity, bonding, attachment, and a sense of belonging and loyalty!

Recognition & Affirmation

The individual who prefers this Language appreciates, is motivated by, and inspired by hearing positive things about their work and effort. Remember... leaders make statements about work and effort... not about them as a person, their style of dress, how they look, etc. These positive statements are also best made in-person, at work, or through a work email... not on your through your personal email or text during... and especially not after work hours. This mistake can lead you and them down a path to HR (Human Resources) or worse. Be Mindful... statements of recognition and affirmation are about your people's work, their effort, and enhancing and protecting Work/Life Harmony for you, them, and the organization!

Being an employee or on a team can be hard work! So much of what makes the organization successful is done behind the senses, not very glamourous, and pounded out in Cubicle Island, behind closed doors, over endless phone calls, and numerous corresponding emails. Recognizing an individual for their efforts and affirming their ability and dedication is not only useful but powerful to this person receiving it!

Knowledge & Advancement

The individual that enjoys this Language wants to know what you know and may want to be YOU someday; meaning they want your spot, your position, your title, your success! This is the hungry new quarterback that wants to soak up all the information from the veteran quarterback they intend to replace. This is the new employee or executive that asks all those questions and is in sponge-mode, because one day your corner office will be their corner office. This person is Motivated and Inspired and needs to be fed!

In speaking with this individual it's important to put your teacher's hat on and be mindful to impart lessons, tips, and tricks of the trade; all the while understanding their goal and sharing the reasons why you're teaching them what you're teaching. The Leader's Questions you learned earlier in this book would be of value here. "How can I best be of service to you?", "Let me know if you need anything.", "How do you learn best?". In the next chapter, we'll get into how to best motivate and have the difficult conversations!

Incentives

This is my wife! She is the best employee, worker, and person I know. She is Knowledge & Advancement and Incentives. She wants to know what you know so she can advance to where she wants to be… and if there is an incentive: a bonus, a competition, something that can be earned that will increase her status at work and our financial well-being… she's all in and cannot be stopped!

The individuals who enjoy this Language like the "Dangling Carrot" and are motivated by raises, bonuses, earned trips, and/or office competitions. So... Offer them! Every company and team has a budget... some bigger and some smaller than others. If raises and bonuses are out of the question... maybe it's time off or gift cards for your people to use in the community with their loved ones.

I've found most people will accept more money, but don't except it. The response I heard most in asking employees and athletes what they wanted from their leadership was... time away from their craft... time away to spend with the people they love. Let's GIVE them that! The bonus is they (and their family) will remember you, the company, or the team when they are out enjoying themselves and paying for it with a gift card they earned from the organization. For example, when the waiter comes with the bill and that employee or player hands over that gift card... You, the company, or the team will graciously and positively be on their mind! Boom... enhancing Work/Life Harmony!

Flexibility

The Language of Flexibility is two-fold. This individual values being able to do their work in a flexible manner; allowing them the ability to move more freely (physically and idea wise). Perhaps having a flexible schedule where they can work in-office, out of office, or at home is most attractive to them. This is me... I hate boxes. This is the running joke in our home... that I hate boxes!

Or, the person would enjoy their ideas for the company or team flexibly implemented into the functioning of the organization. So many companies or teams don't ask for ideas, some ask and don't implement the ideas; discouraging their people from ever speaking up again. This is a dangerous and destructive road as this consistent act will eventually drain the spirit of your "Inspired & Motivated", the "New & Unknown", and eventually the "Steady Steams"; leaving you with the negative version of the "Here, but Not Here's" and "Grouches"!

Note: If an individual selects Flexibility as their Language; ask for clarification... do they want to work in a flexible manner, or do they what their ideas flexibly implemented, or both? The next chapter will shed more light on how to speak this Language of Flexibility in casual times and those dreaded tough conversations. Of course, there are limitations to flexibility in every organization and not everyone can handle flexibility, but where there can be flexibility... can it be?

Respect

Respect is one of my top two languages. At this stage of my life, I'm Flexibility and Respect. I say at this stage of my life... because our Languages change as who we are, where we are in life, and what we want out of life changes. Therefore, it's important to add this to your interview and evaluation process; then ask again every year! When I developed these Languages; I thought everyone would pick one language and Respect. To my surprise, that was not the case... it was just the case for me!

However, Respect turned out to be the BIGGEST Language. What I mean is, people provided the widest array of examples for what respect looked like and felt like. This makes sense as organizations or teams are made up of unique personalities with various pasts, present experiences, and cultures. Here's the List of how workers and teams stated they wanted to be respected (Of course I added a few of my own!):

- Do I have the proper tools in order to be successful?
- Tone of voice
- Ask don't demand... as the boss or leader, the badge of authority is easy to hold up as a last resort. Ask the people following your lead to do a task first.
- Speak at a person's physical level; not standing directly over them giving orders; making them feel small, insignificant, and powerless.

- When giving hard-to-hear feedback be mindful of your seat/ standing position in the room. Do not stand directly in front of the person and inadvertently block a doorway (allowing them to exit quickly if they feel it necessary); making the person feel small, threatened, and trapped. Rather, be sure THEIR is back to the doorway, you are at a 45-degree angle, and either both of you are sitting or standing… or you are sitting (preferably not behind your desk). Everyone knows you're the boss… we don't have to continuously prove it! It says a lot to the person and about you as a leader when we can remove ourselves from the throne to meet another person where they are. A King or Queen is still King or Queen whether their butt is physically sitting on the throne or not!

- Emails—This is huge. I know… as a Leader, you're inundated ALL DAY with emails! Who has time to write a respectful email and send it at the appropriate times? If you're reading this book and reading it to evolve…. YOU DO! It amazes and appalls me how managers, supervisors, and directors send short, snippy, cutting, and sometimes even short-handed coded emails to their people and then expect their people's best work, effort, and loyalty. Could you be short, sharp, rude, and have no time to begin and end your statement with a pleasantry to your spouse, friend, or kids and expect great things to happen or a great relationship? So, why would you do this to your people and Dreamleaders… and if your answer is because you pay them or something to that effect… either you won't be paying them for long or you'll turn your great employees into drones and your bad employees into the majority in your organization; instead of the minority.

  Tip: Start your emails with a positive: "Hi _____, I hope all is well…" "Hi _____ Happy Wednesday, …." (this is my favorite!). Try ending with… "Thank You and enjoy your day" or "I look forward to hearing from you". These can be Copy &

Pasted" or even saved into your signature. Get creative... more importantly, get positive and make it your own!

In the Language of "Respect", emails are best sent during the workday or working hours! As a former business owner and now "Solo-Preneur", I know the grind of waking early or staying up late to get things done, crossing things off the list, sharing ideas, and proposals with others. However, 2:00am is not the time for that email... for two reasons.

Anxiety is on the rise as a crippling epidemic; especially with our younger generation. When their phone rings, dings, chimes or whatever... it can create pressure to respond. The mere sound of the ding; may signify work infringing on their Work/Life Harmony and introducing (however subtle) anxiety and stress. Second, we have no idea of the issues our people are living with regarding their intimate relationships. Do you really want to be the "Ding" or email/text notification your people are arguing about at 2:00am; all because you couldn't wait?

- Manners are Timeless—This is self-explanatory... remember your "Pleases and Thank You's". Do you remember the last time someone didn't say "Please" or "Thank You" to you? We don't want our people feeling that way about us!
- Body Language—What we say is important... Even more so is how we say it and what we look like before, during, and after we say it! I once had a boss that looked so miserable walking into work; greeting everyone with a drained sigh. He looked drained, unhappy about life in and outside of work, and stressed regarding the "Get-To's" of his position; making it undesirable and draining for staff to come in and give it their all or wanting to advance in the company. If that's what moving up in the company looks like and does to you... and what upper management allows... No Thank You!

The basics of body language cannot be ignored: looking at the person when speaking to them, arms at your side and not crossed or on your hips, and remembering to show that awesome smile of yours!

- Loyalty is a Two-Way Street—I wrote about this in my book, *7 Ways to Love*; most leaders that cry their people aren't loyal, typically haven't created an environment worth staying loyal to! Be mindful of the "Whys", needs, and languages of your people and good things tend to happen. We no longer live in a generation where people stay at the same place for 30-40 years. It has to be OK that people leave! How they leave, what they think when they leave, and what they say when they leave is what matters; as the organization or team can be heavily impacted by the "New & Unknowns" they refer back!
- The Red Folder—This is the final stroke of how to earn your title as leader. Can your people come to you with news that is hard for YOU to hear; explaining in-house problems and deficiencies... some of which may be about YOU or your decisions or inaction? Can they trust you will hear them out with an inquisitive mindset and diligence to improve? If the answer is "Yes", great! If not... it's pride-swallowing time; as it's important not to let your evolution as a leader elevate your ego!

There are your Leader's 7! Remember, as leaders... we need to be able to speak all seven, but each of your people have a top one or two. Now that you know what the 7 are... it's important to know what you are... as well as what you're not!

As I mentioned earlier, I'm Flexibility and Respect. I want to be able to work in a flexible manner, implement my ideas, and am huge on giving respect and being in respectful relationships. However, I wasn't always Flexibility and Respect. Early in my career, I was Knowledge & Advancement and Respect; wanting to know what my bosses knew ... so one day I could be them.

Knowing which Language YOU are is important as it will identify who you will bond most easily with and deem most valuable on your team. If you're Incentives... you will gravitate to and enjoy the people who are motivated by that, earn the incentives, and win the competitions. It's human nature... however, it's also easy to discount the efforts of people that speak or benefit from a different language; making them feel unnoticed and less important.

When I was young, I remember getting all A's on my report card. I was so proud... I brought the report card home to my mom and asked, "Can I get something for getting all A's". I forget what I asked for; therefore, it couldn't have been that important. I remember my mom retorting, "I don't give you money to do what you're supposed to do". It sounds harsh, but knowing my mom, it wasn't said in a demeaning way to hurt me, break my spirit, or diminish my efforts. It was simply her stance on rewards. Incentives was not one of her top two languages! Perhaps that why the concept of "Incentives" is a Language that resonates the least with me. Even when I was a Mental Health Therapist, Rewards as a useful intervention were always a last thought or even a last resort; as it wasn't on my mind and it took intentional effort to recognize it as a strategic option.

I share this story to ask you... of The Leader's 7, which are your Top 2? Which two resonate with you the least... not that you don't like, understand, or appreciate their value... but simply resonate the least with you?

1. *Goodies Time*
2. *Quality Minutes*
3. *Recognition & Affirmation*
4. *Knowledge & Advancement*
5. *Incentives*
6. *Flexibility*
7. *Respect*

The two you resonate the least with will tend to be the people you struggle most to enjoy, resonate with the least, or... at the minimum encourage the least! But now you won't have to guess what language they speak or need... you'll know and be proactive and prepared. At the end of this book; you'll receive information on how to retrieve a quick and easy hand-out or email to give to your people; allowing you and your leaders to speak everyone's' in your organization!

CHAPTER 49

Speaking the Leader's 7
In Casual Conversations and
in those "Tough Conversations"

S o, now that you know the 7 Languages... and have the newfound ability to speak everyone's language on the planet, but more importantly... the ability to positively impact everyone that is following you... how do you actually speak it? It's important to speak The 7 in casual times as you pass by in the hallways at work, while visiting cubicles, or in those emails we discussed. Being mindful and consistent in using The 7 in the casual times will work to better motivate and impact your people. It will also make it easier... not easy... but easier to have those "Tough Conversations" most leaders would prefer not to have, but must have in order to stay a leader! As you continue reading, you will see the Casual and Tough ways to speak The Leader's 7 for each language.

"Goodies" Time

Casual Conversation:

"Goodies" Time doesn't have to be verbal; rather a gesture of kindness. Bring something in or treat your employees, team, or person to coffee, pizza, doughnuts, lunch, candy, etc. This can be something you do regularly or impromptu. Yes, some of your people can come to expect such treatment and take your kindness for granted, but not always the people who speak the language of "Goodie" Time! Impromptu has its advantages! Remember the story earlier in the book, when my former supervisor suggested a field trip to the café and treated the team to coffee? That's a spontaneous "Goodies" Time WOW Moment your team will remember and be grateful for!

Tough Conversation:

The "Tough Conversation" suggests that a person you're leading has or continuously engages in actions that go against the vision, mission, and expectations of what you and the organization are instilling. Since you know their language is "Goodies" Time... Bring in, offer, and/or have ready: water, coffee, food, etc. and begin with the You Evolving Now Preface Statement:

1. "Hi _____, can we talk? Remember when I said, one day I may have something to say to you that may be hard for you to hear?
2. Are you ready?
   a. Allow them to brace for impact!
   b. Utilize the Positive Sandwich: what have they done good, state the issue, ask what can be done, share your ideas, problem solve, thank them for allowing you to have the conversation:
3. "It's great having you on the team and you've been great at _____. Lately, I've noticed _____.

Can you help me to understand why this is happening and if there is a way I/we can be of help? *Note: As a leader, the goal in speaking The Leader's 7 in "Tough Conversations" is to be inquisitive; not accusatory!*

Let them answer the question—Remember, they may share information you had no idea of; regarding personal issues, work-related issues, or issues related to unrealistic rules and procedures involving poor leadership. Or, you may simply find they have been taking advantage of the system and are only doing what they've been allowed to do. They are late all the time because leadership has allowed them to be! When this is the case… accept full responsibility, share things have changed, and state the new expectations!

Restate the Plan

1. "Ok, so we are on the same page, from now on you/we are going to_____?
   a. Thank Them
2. "Thanks for letting me have this conversation with you. I wasn't sure how it was going to go. Not everyone handles these conversations the way you did".

Quality Minutes

Casual Conversation:

Ask Great Questions:

- "How are you doing today?"
- "How was your evening?"
- "Do you have plans for tonight?"
- "Did you see the: game, movie, etc.?" and share why you liked it!
- "Do you have plans for the weekend, the summer, the holiday, etc.?"

Tough Conversation:

1. "Hi _____, can we talk? Remember when I said, one day I may have something to say to you that may be hard for you to hear?

2. Are you ready?
   a. Allow them to brace for impact!
   b. Utilize the Positive Sandwich: what have they done good, state the issue, ask what can be done, share your ideas, problem solve, thank them for allowing you to have the conversation:

3. "It's great having you on the team and you've been great at _____. Lately, I've noticed _____. Can you help me to understand why this is happening and if there is a way I/we can be of help? *Note: As a leader, the goal in speaking The Leader's 7 in "Tough Conversations" is to be inquisitive; not accusatory!*

Let them answer the question—Remember, they may share information you had no idea of; regarding personal issues, work-related issues, or issues related to unrealistic rules and procedures involving poor leadership. Or, you may simply find they have been taking advantage of the system and are only doing what they have been allowed to do.

Restate the Plan:

1. "Ok, so we are on the same page, from now on you/we are going to_____?
   a. Thank Them

2. "Thanks for letting me have this conversation with you. I wasn't sure how it was going to go. Not everyone handles these conversations the way you did".

Knowledge & Advancement

Casual Conversation:

- "Let me know if there's anything you need from me?"
- "Are you comfortable with everything or have any questions?"
- "I'd like to show you how to do _____ in case I'm not around?"
- "What do you want to get out of your experience being here at ___ (company/team)___?". "How can I help?"

Tough Conversation:

Informal:

1. "You mentioned Knowledge and Advancement was important to you, let me show you _____ so you know what you need to know for next time".

Formal:

1. "Hi _____, can we talk? Remember when I said, one day I may have something to say to you that may be hard for you to hear?
2. Are you ready?
   a. Allow them to brace for impact!
   b. Utilize the Positive Sandwich: what have they done good, state the issue, ask what can be done, share your ideas, problem solve, thank them for allowing you to have the conversation:
3. "It's great having you on the team and you've been great at _____. You mentioned your Language is Knowledge & Advancement, it's going to be hard to advance if _____ continues. Can you help me to understand why this is happening? Remember... Inquisitive; not accusatory!

Let them answer the question—Remember, they may share information you had no idea of; regarding personal issues, work-related issues, or issues related to unrealistic rules and procedures involving poor leadership. Or, you may simply find they have been taking advantage of the system and are only doing what they have been allowed to do.

Restate the Plan:

1. "Ok, so we are on the same page, from now on you/we are going to_____?
   a. Thank Them
2. "Thanks for letting me have this conversation with you. I wasn't sure how it was going to go. Not everyone handles these conversations the way you did".

Recognition & Affirmation

Casual Conversation:

- "Hey_____, great job with _____!"
- "Just wanted you to know I/we appreciate you doing _____!"
- "Thank you for_____, it was a big help and made a big difference!"

Tough Conversation:

Remember, don't use the Bully Word, "but"; as this person tends to struggle the most with criticism... harsh or constructive:

1. "Hi _____, can we talk? Remember when I said, one day I may have something to say to you that may be hard for you to hear?
2. Are you ready?
   a. Allow them to brace for impact!
   b. Utilize the Positive Sandwich: what have they done good, state the issue, ask what can be done, share your ideas,

problem solve, thank them for allowing you to have the conversation:

3. "It's great having you on the team and you've been great at _____. You mentioned your Language is Recognition & Affirmation, it's going to be hard for me to continue to do that if _____ continues. Can you help me to understand why this is happening? Remember... Inquisitive; not accusatory!

Let them answer the question—Remember, they may share information you had no idea of; regarding personal issues, work-related issues, or issues related to unrealistic rules and procedures involving poor leadership. Or, you may simply find they have been taking advantage of the system and are only doing what they have been allowed to do.

Restate the Plan:

1. "Ok, so we are on the same page, from now on you/we are going to_____?
   a. Thank Them
2. "Thanks for letting me have this conversation with you. I wasn't sure how it was going to go. Not everyone handles these conversations the way you did".

Incentives

Casual Conversation:

- As a leader... offer contests, prizes, raises, rewards, bonuses, etc. to your team
- How are you making out with__(the incentive)___?

Tough Conversation:

Informal:

1. "Hi_____, I want you to be able to earn your _____, let's discuss how we can get you there or at least in a better position.

Formal:

1. "Hi _____, can we talk? Remember when I said, one day I may have something to say to you that may be hard for you to hear?

2. Are you ready?
   a. Allow them to brace for impact!
   b. Utilize the Positive Sandwich: what have they done good, state the issue, ask what can be done, share your ideas, problem solve, thank them for allowing you to have the conversation:

3. "It's great having you on the team and you've been great at _____. You mentioned your Language is Incentives. It's going to be hard to earn your _____...
   if _____ continues. Can you help me to understand why this is happening? Remember... Inquisitive; not accusatory!

Let them answer the question—Remember, they may share information you had no idea of; regarding personal issues, work-related issues, or issues related to unrealistic rules and procedures involving poor leadership. Or, you may find they have lost interest in the incentive for a variety of reasons: they fell too far behind, are managing other pressing issues, or their Language changed due to life circumstances.

Restate the Plan:

1. "Ok, so we are on the same page, from now on you/we are going to_____? Great!"
   a. Thank Them

2. "Thanks for letting me have this conversation with you. I wasn't sure how it was going to go. Not everyone handles these conversations the way you did".

Flexibility

Casual Conversation:

- "Is there anything you need?"
- "How do you think things are going?"
- "I'd like to know what you think; what's going great here and what's going bad here?

Tough Conversation:

Informal:

- "Hi _____. Can we talk? I know flexibility is important to you, we have to create win-wins for everyone in this situation, this is my/our position_____. How do we make this a win-win?
- "Hi _____. Can we talk? Unfortunately, we can no longer continue how things have been going. We need _____, how can we make this happen to create a win-win?

Formal:

1. "Hi _____, can we talk? Remember when I said one, day I may have something to say to you that may be hard for you to hear?
2. Are you ready?
   a. Allow them to brace for impact!
   b. Utilize the Positive Sandwich: what have they done good, state the issue, ask what can be done, share your ideas, problem solve, thank them for allowing you to have the conversation:
3. "It's great having you on the team and you've been great at _____. You mentioned your Language is Flexibility, that's going to be hard to continue if _____

continues. Can you help me to understand why this is happening? Remember... Inquisitive; not accusatory!

Let them answer the question—Remember, they may share information you had no idea of; regarding personal issues, work-related issues, or issues related to unrealistic rules and procedures involving poor leadership. Or, you may simply find they have been taking advantage of the system and are only doing what they have been allowed to do.

Restate the Plan:

1. "Ok, so we are on the same page, from now on you/we are going to_____? Great!".
   a. Thank Them
2. "Thanks for letting me have this conversation with you. I wasn't sure how it was going to go. Not everyone handles these conversations the way you did".

Respect

Casual Conversation:

- Daily Connection: Smile, Say Hello, DO and BE your best, Controlled Venting, and at times be willing to the dirty work of the job along with your people as a leader!

Tough Conversation:

1. "Hi _____, can we talk? Remember when I said, one day I may have something to say to you that may be hard for you to hear?
2. Are you ready?
   a. Allow them to brace for impact!
   b. Utilize the Positive Sandwich: what have they done good, state the issue, ask what can be done, share your ideas,

problem solve, thank them for allowing you to have the conversation:

3. "It's great having you on the team and you've been great at _____. Lately, I've noticed _____. Can you help me to understand why this is happening? Remember... Inquisitive; not accusatory!

Let them answer the question—Remember, they may share information you had no idea of; regarding personal issues, work-related issues, or issues related to unrealistic procedures involving protocol and leadership. Or, you may simply find they have been taking advantage of the system and are only doing what they have been allowed to do.

Restate the Plan:

1. "Ok, so we are on the same page, from now on you/we are going to_____?
   a. Thank Them
2. "Thanks for letting me have this conversation with you. I wasn't sure how it was going to go. Not everyone handles these conversations the way you did".

Note: After speaking the 7 and thanking them for the conversation; great leaders (executive or employee) protect themselves. The best way is to send a follow-up email describing the conversation and the agreed-upon plan of action moving forward; being sure to start and end the email with the same positivity and hope as the conversation! Unfortunately in the world of business, a great conversation never happened without having it in black & white.... Be Mindful!

Congrats!!! Now you know how to speak The Leader's 7 to your people and teams to impact, influence, protect, and build! The concepts and examples work for me and countless others. Enjoy your evolution and newfound ability to connect with the significant people in your day-to-day! Connect with me at andre@youevolvingnow.com to receive an easy-to-use one-page email version of The Leader's 7 to print out for your team!

CHAPTER 50

The Evolving Pyramid

Now that you know and have begun to master the 7 Ways to Lead... let's start building your team. I often share this concept during on-site speaking engagements or my EVOLVE & Lead Program for companies as it's the best and easiest way to build a positive and motivated team from within your organization! I know... you may already be on a team, have a team, or your company already has teams in place. However, you are creating YOUR team, full of "The Inspired & Motivated", and this process can be used at work, on a sports team, or in your personal life for the purpose of EVOLVING! Remember, in businesses and teams, there are "The Inspired & Motivated"; the people that maximize the use of their time to not only complete a task; but WOW the task, have vision and ambition, are idea-based, problem-solvers, and are super driven! However, most businesses and teams will stay average because they only have one or very few of these individuals. The company and team may excel for a short while; but, in time, burn this individual out only to replace them with the next bright-eyed willing soul to accept the position.

These same companies and teams are also host to "The Grouches". These individuals can drain the energy out of the room, the mission, and the daily experience as they are negative, complainers, and seek ways to get by doing the bare minimum. The two important questions regarding both individuals are:

1. Why are they here? What do they want to get out of the experience?
2. How can we spread "Inspired & Motivated", without demanding people to operate at this level; rather creating an environment where they are willing to give, do, and be more... creating a culture of positivity and excellence?

Question 1 may seem silly to explore, "Why are they there?". In my experience, the "Inspired & Motivated" are simply wired that way and would be that way no matter where they are. They may come from a culture of hard work, perfectionism, or task-completion; therefore, they value work-ethic and how their positive output enhances their self-worth, reputation, and advancement. Other reasons may include they enjoy receiving recognition, want incentives, or simply don't like staying still in their mind or body and rather be productive in achieving their definition of success for themselves and the team.

"The Grouches" reason can vary as well. Maybe their consistent negative attitude is due to life issues, health issues, or existing poor leadership practices such as constantly changing direction, poor communication, lack of discipline, favoritism, micro-managing, making decisions without consulting with the team, requesting and expecting work to be completed during off-times, unrealistic deadlines, etc. All of this... can cause a person to feel stressed, pressed, and obligated to succeed with little help and too many landmines.

So how do we think out-of-the-box to form a team of individuals that want to be positive, move forward, succeed, and EVOLVE? The answer is... The Evolving Pyramid! Imagine yourself at work or on your team. Think... who are the two or three people you trust and respect most... that get their job done, do it great, answer questions you have, and are always willing? Boom... you now have your team!

What is their superpower; what are they great at, what are you impressed by, and how does your trust in them and their superpower make your job easier? Do they know how you feel? Your homework is to let them know? I always suggest an old fashion brief conversation of affirming them and thanking them, but the power of e-mail works just as well.

Note: Face-to-Face and work e-mail work best done during work hours; allowing them a gift of appreciation while at work, time to process your kind words, and time to respond if they choose. I'd refrain from texting and off-hour texting as the person is on their personal time, with their loved ones, and things can become misconstrued; suddenly changing you from a great person to a possible problem in their person-life, home-life, or intimate relationship. Keep it professional and on professional time; you don't want that issue!

Now that you have your team... let's invite and meet consistently. To start it can be daily, three times per week, but no less than one time per week. The meeting is meant to be brief... quality over quantity! The purpose is to build... build communication, respect, drive, vision, purpose, and a process! Start the meeting with... The purpose... Thank them for attending and "Why" they are there; sharing they were selected due to their positivity, work-ethic, knowledge-base, and willingness to win the day! Next, do "Your Positive of the Week!". Since the group is small... everyone gets to answer, "What's been you positive of the week?". This is awesome because the answer, typically, has nothing to do with their work, their sport, etc... rather real-life stuff you typically wouldn't know the answer to and couldn't have guessed; allowing more personal bonds as you get to see each other as humans with real lives and various roles as people, partners, parents, professionals, and more!

The first meeting is set to explain why you want to put together a team of great individuals interested in being their best and doing their best to make things as great as they can be. Ask each person:

1. Thanks, them for attending and explain why each person was invited to join The Evolving Pyramid!
2. Why are you here at the job or on the team? Typically, this is only asked during our initial interview… our "Whys" can change!
3. What do they love most about their job?
4. What Language do they prefer (The Leader's 7)?
5. What's their Dream… and how can we help if possible?
6. Explain the purpose is to meet consistently, regularly, and purposefully
7. Use these questions for the eventual newcomers that are invited to enter the group; as the purpose is to keep Evolving the Pyramid! You are at the top and the pyramid gets wider as other positive influencers are invited in.

As I mentioned earlier, the meetings are not meant to be long but are most beneficial when operated in this order:

1. Positive of the Week (P. O. W.)—give each person 30 seconds. As the group grows… perhaps only 5-7 people get to share. Note: Everyone must clap for a person when they conclude. If you're not a professional athlete or someone that's on stage often, when was the last time you think a person was applauded for? Give them that gift! Believe me… you're going to like it when it's your turn! Also, the P. O. W. is the first thing you will be tempted to eliminate due to your busy day… DON'T DO IT! This is what's creating that personal bond within your

team… and the part they enjoy the most as they get to see their teammates as more than just professionals. Protocol Meetings don't do that!

2. "Thank You for attending and all you do!"—Thank your team for their efforts and willingness to be a part of the vision!

3. "Opportunity of the Week?"—What is the opportunity and area of focus for the week? Language is important here; "Opportunity" rather than "Problem". The important thing is the room is filled with "The Inspired & Motivated" and not "The Grouches", but negativity can always find a way to seep in. As the leader, it's your job to influence positive and success language!

4. "How can I be of help"—Perhaps the team has the new opportunities under control, perhaps they have a question you can answer, or the team can provide a new perspective and path for success. The point is they now know they're not alone and there are several leaders that could be of assistance.

5. Professional Goal of the Week!—"What is everyone's professional goal for the week?". "The Inspired & Motivated", "Steady Streams", and sometimes the "Here, but Not Here's" will do their job, but can easily get caught being busy instead of better. "Better" is having a professional goal for the week and being willing to put that in the front of our mind and in our daily calendar!

6. The Leader's 7—"Who have you done the Leader's 7 with this week and how's it going?". This protects your leaders, the organization, the team, and The Leader's 7 from the "Busy" Bully! When your team knows they will consistently be asked something… they tend to have an answer ready for you. The Leader's 7 has now become a positive expectation of caring for our people! Note: Use the Leader's 7 in the Evolving Pyramid Meetings… don't forget to gift the attendees with their Language!

7. Recap & Close!—Thank everyone and briefly recap what was discussed. It's amazing how much can be forgotten within just a few minutes! Conclude with… "Please feel free to come to me if you need anything or if I can be of service.". One of the few rules I maintain as a leader is… please accompany your problem with a suggested solution! We may use your solution if it's reasonable, doable, and fair. We may combine ideas or may not be able to use your idea; as there may be a bigger-picture-issue you are not aware of. As a leader, this saves you from becoming the "All-the-Time Problem Solver"; never able to get anything done but solving problems all day. It also allows your team to think, grow, evolve, and become!

After several <u>consistent</u> weeks… as anything must happen consistently and purposefully for it to work… we are now ready to expand the Evolving Pyramid. Remember the people you trusted and invited in? Who do they trust? Why? What are their superpowers? How do they make life easier for them? Invite them to the meeting. This is how we expand and grow positivity, purpose, vision, and leadership; especially in a culture that may be negative, fractured, or apathetic!

Start small, with the willing, and expand! With consistency and purpose… this will grow and the individuals that don't belong will show themselves. This group can get BIG… as long as it's consistent, positive, purposeful, and makes the people in it and outside of it better! Lastly: In setting the date for your Evolving Pyramid… I've found the optimum day to be Tuesday; not competing with the tired Mondays, Hump-Day, or later in the weekdays in which people are counting down to the weekend. Pick your day and time and do it *consistently*; making it a pleasant and positive expectation of growth!

Thank You for reading, I look forward to connecting with you, and enjoy your EVOLUTION!!!

Are you interested in enhancing your Leadership and Work/Life Harmony? Then 7 Ways to Lead is for you!

If you're interested in enhancing your Leadership and Work / Life Harmony, *7 Ways to Lead* is for you! Whether you are in a professional position of leadership or a leader of your own life; 7 Ways to Lead shares common sense and easy to use insight to enhance your personal leadership and effective leadership skills. The number one complaint from many companies is, "Our leaders don't know how to lead!". Why would they? Most people are promoted because they did one thing really well or outlasted their "addicted to average" co-workers/teammates; not because they knew how to lead! My favorite example is, "You sold a million dollars worth of product... You are now the Sales Manager!". They haven't proved they can manage or lead anyone; they've only proven they can sell a million dollars worth of product... their way!

Lastly, Work / Life Harmony is more important now than it's ever been! The notion of leaving home at the door before entering work and leaving work at the door before entering home is obsolete! The fact we all have cell phones means our significant other, all of our relationships, and outside life now enter work with us... ALL DAY! So, when things are bad intimately, parentally, and socially it shows up at work; with employees trying to do their job in between responding to ten pages of "Hate Texts"! In contrast, when that same employee returns home, their phone may continue to ring, ding, or chime with work emails, work texts, etc. If they respond; they've effectively communicated it's ok to invade their time. If they don't, it doesn't erase the anxiety of not responding or knowing a pile of work is building up. We may not find a true balance between both realms, but we can and we must find and create harmony between the two. 7 Ways to Lead helps. Enjoy your EVOLUTION!!! *www.youevolvingnow.com*

CPSIA information can be obtained
at www.ICGtesting.com
Printed in the USA
LVHW050301110921
697499LV00004B/11